Any mother who can motivate her children to eagerly volunteer to work around the house must be doing something right!

Marjorie King Garrison believes that discipline, honor, ingenuity, humor, a sense of adventure, and hard work are all integral parts of the package called "happy family."

THE RECIPE IS ALL HERE: the basic rules of enjoying your family ... molding character in your children ... disciplining and training from babyhood ... becoming happy parents (and creating a lifelong love affair) ... how to keep that first baby from becoming a tyrant ... preconditioning a child to succeed academically as well as socially ... learning with your teens ... building family traditions, and more.

Happy Families Are Homemade

Marjorie King Garrison

David C. Cook Publishing Co.
ELGIN, ILLINOIS—WESTON, ONTARIO

HAPPY FAMILIES ARE HOMEMADE

David C. Cook Publishing Co., Elgin, IL 60120
Printed in the United States of America
Library of Congress Catalog Number: 75-18922
ISBN: 0-912692-804

Dedicated to my husband, Irving,
who keeps romance in our marriage,
and to our five children
who are a product of that marriage—
Marilynne, Sharon, David, Kathleen and Bob.

Grateful acknowledgment is made for permission to reprint the following chapters:

Chapter 1 from "Front Rank," April 16, 1972; Chapter 3 from "Hearthstone," November, 1959; Chapter 4 from "Christian Home," June, 1964; Chapter 7 from "Hearthstone," May, 1959; Chapter 13 from "Hearthstone," March, 1962; Chapter 15 from "Hearthstone," February, 1963; Chapter 16 from "Hearthstone," January, 1963; Chapter 18 from "Christian Home," February, 1962; Chapter 20 from "Christian Home," November, 1953; Chapter 21 from "Hearthstone," January, 1965; Chapter 24 from "Hearthstone," April, 1962.

FOREWORD

Every day, as a licensed marriage, family, and child counselor, I meet with people whose family lives seem to be shattered. Whatever the cause or causes for this, I have noticed one basic fact regarding those who come to me for counseling—they have ceased to enjoy being in their family. That fact is so obvious that there is certainly nothing profound about it. Yet, it does point out that we parents sometimes have such great expectations of ourselves and our children, and we sometimes try so hard at parenting that we forget that family life can be happy and fulfilling. I will even say that it should be.

Certainly there is more to family life today than the basic need for physical and economic survival, in contrast to the situation just a few generations ago. The human needs that result in family units have in fact been shifting rather rapidly away from physical survival to emotional and spiritual survival. Thus today we have more expectations of family life.

This book is a blend of actual experiences, sound psychology, and practical suggestions regarding enjoyable, yet fulfilling family life. The author knows what she's talking about when she writes about how to have a happy family. In contrast to some authors on the subject, she has a family of her own. Her grasp of family dynamics is apparent in the many practical suggestions that are presented. But it is more than just good advice on parenting. It presents an experienced perspective of abundant living in the best sense of the word.

I am fortunate to have been a part of the author's family—as her brother, brother-in-law to her husband, and uncle to their five children. For many years I have observed what a happy life the Garrison family has together. In the final analysis, the test of any approach to effective family life is "does it work?" I see living evidence that family life as discussed by the author does work.

I used to say, "Marge, you ought to write a book about family living." I'm glad she finally did.

San Diego, California   DR. ROBERT R. KING, JR.
Executive Director
College Avenue Counselling Center

CONTENTS

Preface

1. *Stop for the View*   15

2. *To Spank or Not to Spank*   21

3. *I Don't Want My Child to Have Every Advantage*   27

4. *Does Your Husband Have a Place in Your Life?*   33

5. *What's the Gimmick?*   37

6. *Why Not Use Camp Techniques in the Home?*   43

7. *Do Your Children Work for You?*   47

8. *Reevaluating Techniques for Today's World*   55

9. *The First Baby*   59

10. *Keep Your Eye Upon the Doughnut*   65

11. *First Things First*   73

12. *Hi, Juniors!*   79

13. *I'm Not Jealous of Teenagers*   85

14. *What Teenagers Think of Adults*   91

15. *Up and Down*   97

16. *Love Your Teenager*   105

17. *Understanding Parents of Teenagers (and Yourself Too!)*   109

18. *Plan for When the Birds Start Flying*   115

19. *Traditions Can Be Fun*   121

20. *Make Thanksgiving a Tradition*   125

21. *Christmas in Your Heart*   129

22. *Family Year With Meaning*   135

23. *The Family Goes to Church*   141

24. *Are You a Parasite Parent?*   147

25. *It's Worth the Risk*   153

    Reading List   155

PREFACE

It is easy to talk in generalities about how much fun a family is, but how about specifics? Psychologists and home economists do not deal with children on a 24-hour-a-day basis. Life goes beyond picture postcards or the TV glamour of a mother and father surrounded by handsome, well-dressed, adoring children. Children often look like tramps and they frequently aren't adoring. A book concerned only with generalities is about as valuable as a cookbook with no recipes. However, techniques for dealing with people are not as easy to follow as a recipe.

Parents can pool findings, but what works with one child may not work with another, and what is suitable for our family may not be suitable for yours. All children are different. However, even with children, it helps to have a basic recipe from which to depart. I have started with philosophy and goals and have limited my audience to parents concerned that their children learn ethics and Christian principles. In some cases, I have made a special attempt to clearly link a practical suggestion with the Biblical teaching that gives rise to that suggestion. In other cases, I merely offer what has worked for us, knowing that a base of Christian faith was underlying all our attempts to guide our children toward responsible adulthood.

Today's world is frightening and challenging. With our scientific knowledge, we have the ability to make a decent world for everyone, but we lack the character. Our Western world's problems are more a matter of integrity, morality and concern than plain survival. Perhaps part of the problem is that in the last generation we have not taken homemaking seriously as a profession. Our concern has been to have a higher standard of living rather than to achieve a higher way of life.

If we are to have a better world, it can only come about from better people. What more important contribution can we make than to train children to put God first in their lives and to be concerned about others? There will be sorrows, but joys too as the human family learns to live together. We can do our part in understanding and communication, both in the intimate family and human family. Our children have the right to choose some different values than ours. Every individual differs, and can live with integrity only by his own conscience.

Enjoy your family. Our five children have enriched our lives and given us new insights.

Happy Families Are Homemade

1

Stop for the View

MANY PEOPLE GO THROUGH LIFE like relentless mountain climbers, so absorbed in getting to the top that they don't enjoy the scenery along the way. They long for the day in which they can look over everything from the mountain peak, and when they get there they find the views are no more exhilarating than those they could have had on the upward path.

Too often people are the same way about children. "I can hardly wait until he gets out of the diaper stage. I'm a slave to the washing machine." ... "That's the third vase broken this month. I'll be glad when she gets over being two years old!" ... "How untidy he is, hair never combed and knees always out of his blue jeans. Won't it be wonderful when he gets to be a teenager and is more concerned about his appearance?" ... "How does anyone keep from going insane around teenagers? Noise, noise, noise, all the time. Never think of anyone besides themselves." ... "How do parents avoid going to the poor house when their children are in college? One year of college costs more than I made when I first started to work." . . . "What good does it do to raise a family? They grow up and forget you. Never write. All those years of sacrifice gone."

Haven't you heard each sentiment expressed at some time in your life? If you have a family, you might as well enjoy each stage as it comes along. Otherwise, you'll always be searching for the mountaintop of experience, never realizing that it is to be savored each day. Parenthood itself should be the mountaintop experience, not just the final rocky ledge at the end of the climb as the only source of joy. True, goals are important, both for ourselves and for our children, but not so overwhelming that we don't take time to enjoy each step of the way.

When I had five young children, the oldest still seven, and the mountain of work so big that at times it seemed right on top of me, I was sometimes annoyed to have mothers in their 40's and 50's tell me, "Enjoy this stage while you can. Too soon they grow up and go away from you." I sometimes secretly thought, "If you're so envious, you take over for a day and let me have a vacation."

However, now that three of our children are married, I'm forced to admit there is an element of truth in what they said. Not that I agree with them entirely. They failed to admit that it's exciting to see a child grow up and start her own home. No good mother should want to keep her children from reaching maturity. And as a grandmother, I think there are some tremendous advantages. However, a family is closest when the members are dependent on one another.

There is a brief time, before other factors become important, when much as a child may grumble or try to disobey, he accepts the parent as the fount of all wisdom. Each stage along the way has both liabilities and compensations. The mother who truly enjoys her family must dwell fundamentally on the compensations, although, being human, she may feel there are days when all the liabilities gang up on her.

What are some of the advantages and disadvantages of the average mother? The young baby may fill up the washing machine with diapers and wet sheets, but there is something terrifically exciting about a new life—a promise for the future. During the first year of life, a new baby learns so many things that no parent can fail to notice each accomplishment and rejoice. If a good routine is established, a baby is very little trouble in the early months. You can put him down and he'll stay there; you know where he is.

As a child learns to sit up or crawl, a stroller makes it easier to move him, and a high chair makes it easier to feed him. No longer can you assume that he is safely put down, but he's learning so much that only an indifferent parent could fail to be impressed and proud.

A two-year-old can be into everything, but it is fun to watch his vocabulary increase and his abilities grow. My husband was away during the war when our oldest daughter was two, and he made a scrapbook of clippings from my letters, noting the tremendous amount she learned and the interesting things she did.

The elementary school age is in many respects the easiest of all ages. The child learns both some independence and respect for authority. The family is a close-knit group, and many things are fun to do together. Physically the child is often at his most unattractive stage, but it's wonderful how much he can do and how much he appreciates the family group. Of course, school brings outside responsibilities, like PTA, Camp Fire Girls, Scouts, and Y, but these can all be rewarding experiences. Go to PTA. Help with Camp Fire Girls. This is the time that children want their family to be represented. When he's a teenager, he won't want you to act as if you even know him while in a group.

Although teenage brings an elimination of the problem of baby-sitting and children are old enough to be of considerable help, often this is the most difficult age. Suddenly what you think or say is of no importance at all, and the judgments of fellow teenagers, a favorite teacher or someone else's parents are of overwhelming value. But this belittling of parental ideas and habits is a necessary adjunct to growth and eventual independence, and it's comforting to have other adults tell you what wonderful children you have, even if they seldom display the same side to you.

The adult stage can be the most fascinating one

of all if you have permitted your child to mature and to make his own decisions. You can enjoy each other as friends, accepting each other's faults and limitations as well as virtues.

For the child receiving Christian training, a pattern of spiritual growth can run parallel to his mental and social development. As a preschooler, he can begin learning that God loves him and cares for him in many special ways. During the elementary years, he will be formulating a sense of right and wrong. If he is helped at this time to understand what God says about right and wrong, he will include that in the workings of his conscience. If he hears nothing of it, he will be left to act on the level of the moral standards he sees practiced in the world around him.

Children vary greatly as to when they are personally ready to express their faith in Christ. Leading Christian educators tell us, however, that late elementary or early junior high years are prime time. Parents should do all they can to show their children the joy and reality of Christian belief during this very important developmental stage before the stress of adolescence catches up with them.

The parent who is to enjoy his family needs to be the sort of person who sees a glass of milk as half full, not half empty, a person who dwells on the doughnut, not the hole. Each stage of family life may have its difficulties, but each also has its blessings. Happy are the parents who look on the positive side and enjoy the view along the way.

19

2

To Spank or Not to Spank

IF THIS WERE A PERFECT WORLD with perfect people in it we might need no parents, supervisors, policemen or government. But since it isn't, people in authority are needed, in spite of their mistakes; anarchy is worse.

About the time I was beginning my teaching and parenthood, the permissive type of discipline in the schoolroom and home was in vogue. Psychologists dinned into us the vast harm we could do to a child's psyche by oppressive discipline or by making him do something he didn't want to do. All correction should be done in a positive manner; if something went wrong, it was clearly the fault of the parent or the teacher. The child was never blamed. Most blame was given to the parents because they were responsible both for the heredity and the environment.

I think the disorder and the violence in our world today are partially a result of the permissive training that went on for 25 or 30 years. Too many people have grown up feeling no responsibility for their own actions and believing that if matters did not go their way they should throw a tantrum.

In our education courses we were told to appeal to a child's interest in his reading and in his reports. Nothing was said about seniors who could not yet read at second-grade level. Theory is interesting, but a little experience teaching convinced me that if the majority of the class was to learn anything, there had to be order. Some students can be cajoled into good behavior; others need some show of authority.

Any parent makes mistakes, but by the time our youngest son was a senior in high school, I was even more convinced of my original premise. It is better to err on the side of being too strict than of being too permissive. It is possible to cite examples of children of too strict parents as well as too permissive parents who have gone wrong, but we have far more unhappy and purposeless adults who were overindulged as children. It is easier, in a classroom or in a home, to ease up on discipline that is too strict than it is to tighten up when things are out of hand.

Basically, the purpose of discipline is to develop self-discipline so a child grows up to be a dependable adult who can make his own decisions. Good people are as much a result of training as are good musicians. They don't just happen. Parents who really love their children will take the time, effort and willpower to help them develop self-discipline. Children who were obnoxious two-year-olds are often obnoxious teenagers. If a child does not learn discipline when he is younger, he usually makes himself and those around him unhappy as he grows older.

Young people may protest against certain rules and regulations; but if the rules are fair and reasonable, they will accept them.

I want to emphasize the importance of using reasonable discipline. To be effective, discipline must be reasonable to the child, not just to the parent. The parent may know very well that a child deserves to be disciplined, but if the child does not understand why he should be disciplined or if the discipline does not fit the behavior problem, the result is certain to be anger and frustration.

Parents have been directly warned in the Bible against letting that happen. "Do not provoke your children to anger." Unreasonable discipline will do just that. But sensible and understandable Christian discipline will produce a happy child as well as a happy parent.

All our children, even the boys, have done baby-sitting for the neighbors. They have looked after some neighbor children since they were born. Once their favorite baby-sitting jobs were with families who offered them soft drinks or cookies; but soon their favorite jobs were with families where the children were trained to mind. Years of baby-sitting have left our children convinced that their own children are going to behave.

Interestingly enough, in the last few years psychologists, educators and columnists have been coming to the same conclusion. You can hardly open a popular magazine without finding some article stressing that children feel unloved and cheated with overpermissive parents.

Stanley Coopersmith, an associate professor of psychology at the Davis Campus of the University of California, says in his book, *The Antecedents of Self-Esteem,* that self-esteem is the most important factor in inoculating children against failure and unhappiness as they grow up. In addition to love and democracy being present in families who develop self-esteem, the parents were significantly less permissive than the parents of children of low esteem. The child of permissive parents feels insecure and that his parents do not love him enough to take the trouble to discipline him.

Self-discipline can be developed from the time a child is born. Every time a parent gives in to a child who is whining, crying or making himself disagreeable, he is training that child to misbehave.

Perhaps these ideas may seem far away from the original question, but they aren't for they are a part of the philosophy used in answering the question. Should a child be spanked? Possibly. It depends on the child and his age. The type of punishment used is not as important as the fact that it is consistent and fair. An occasional spanking may be necessary, but a parent who often has to resort to spankings after a child reaches school age has not done a good job when the child was younger.

Spankings are most effective when a child is too young for reasoning and must learn something for his own safety, such as staying out of the street.

Occasionally when the children were babies and fighting going to sleep, particularly while traveling, I would give them a small spank on the bottom, and they would fall asleep.

Usually isolation was the most effective punishment with our children. They were not permitted to be with other people unless they could be pleasant. When I did something particularly horrible as a child, I was not permitted to read—the worst thing that could happen to me. The punishment needs to fit the child.

Occasionally, when my husband was an elementary principal, he had to spank a child. Usually it was a child who had been programed by his parents to think that authority was shown by spanking. The important thing is that children sense that there are certain standards of behavior acceptable at home or at school. Behavior not meeting those standards should be punished, not rewarded.

Dr. Benjamin Spock says that child psychology cannot substitute for morality. There are more things in life than social adjustment. This paragraph from his book, *Raising Children in a Difficult Time,* is particularly good:

> Good parents should stop worrying, I feel, about whether the strictness of their standards will alienate their children's love or cause maladjustment. Children are made more comfortable in having been kept from wrongdoing or in paying for it. Underneath,

they feel grateful to their parents. Naturally they won't say thank you; they grumble or sulk temporarily; but this doesn't mean they have been disciplined unwisely.

Parent effectiveness training, under the direction of Dr. Thomas Gordon, points out that there are three ways to discipline: (1) the parent wins, (2) the child wins, (3) nobody loses; it's a compromise. Anyone who has worked with people, whether adults or children, realizes that too often we make issues over matters that really aren't important. Solutions that save face often are good. However, there are some issues, all through life, on which I have been unwilling to negotiate. Democracy is important, but so, sometimes, is authority. As one mother put it, "With the high cost of living, I'm not willing to negotiate whether my child wears a raincoat and rubbers on a rainy day."

But with many issues the third way of disciplining is usually more effective. We were strong believers in the family council and often used it to resolve difficult situations. But children old enough for family council are usually too old for spanking. And sometimes my husband would proclaim that not all votes were of equal value. We believe in democracy in the home, but we also believe the home needs a boss or a chairman.

Although imagination, a sense of humor and the light touch can often eliminate the need for punishment, growing good children is like growing a good garden; pruning and trimming are needed.

3

I Don't Want My Child to Have Every Advantage

ELEANOR HAD AN INTERESTED AUDIENCE as she told about the panic her neighbor endured when a teenage daughter ran away from home after being corrected. "And the unjust part of it is," concluded Eleanor, "there was absolutely no reason for the girl to run away. My neighbor had given her *every* advantage."

Every advantage! I don't want my child to have *every advantage*. Why is it that so often parents who have come up the hard way want to spare their children the struggles and problems that gave character to their own lives? I feel that many of the broken marriages, much of the gambling and get-rich-quick schemes, the selfishness and the misery of the world are due to people who, when they were children, were made to feel that life revolved around them.

If it had been my daughter, I would have been even more distressed about her return than about her leaving. For she returned, not because she missed her parents or because she was concerned

27

about hurting them, but because when she lied about her age and got a job, she found the going too tough and disagreeable.

Some things should be every child's birthright: an atmosphere of love, friends, understanding, family fun, beauty and purpose. That doesn't mean that love should have a dollar sign, that friends should be only of a certain class and race, that understanding can come only from highly paid psychologists, dentists, and doctors, or that beauty will come only from exclusive shops.

Children of every social and economic background deserve these birthright experiences, and parents from every social and economic background can provide them. I am sometimes inclined to think that parents of ordinary means have an advantage over people of wealth in doing so, for they may of necessity give their children more of themselves, since they cannot give as much in the way of purchased advantages. An excess of material benefits sometimes makes it doubly hard to communicate true affection between parents and children.

Many of these birthright privileges grow right out of the Christian faith. Let me explain why this is true.

People who have difficulty learning to give and receive real love will learn about love as they come to know God's love in their hearts. In learning to love God, they learn how to love other people, too. And I do not mean merely that the Christian learns to "dutifully love" the non-Christian. That is not what I am talking about. I mean husbands and wives, and parents and children, and brothers and sisters all learn to give and receive love in a wholesome atmosphere that leads to growth and maturity for everyone.

Local congregations are a wonderful source of understanding friends. Oh, we joke a lot about the foibles of our fellow Christians, but we also know that they share a genuine concern for one another's well-being.

All in all, serving Christ can put family members in real touch with one another. It gives them some common beliefs and projects. It gives each person a sense of purpose and meaning through knowing that God has special work for each to do. It is a vital part of family life, a part that contributes much toward making the family unit a success.

People lift their eyebrows when we mention our five children, and often say, "It must be nice to have a big family, but we can't afford it. Food and clothes and college are so expensive now." My husband is a teacher, and while teachers in California make an adequate salary you'd hardly consider them in the luxury class. It's not the five children people can't afford, but the luxuries they want for themselves and their children. Ecology will not help the rest of the world if we spend the surplus on ourselves.

All our children went to college, but we didn't hand them college on a silver platter. Marilynne worked at a caramel corn shop and was a mother's helper during the summers. Sharon helped neighbors and worked summers as a waitress. David did gardening for the neighbors, worked summers and holidays at the post office, and served at banquets and weddings at college. Kathleen spent many hours as a mother's helper to pay as much as she could of her passage to Spain for her first year of college.

My parents always regretted that the depression prevented them from paying all our college expenses. There was no need for regret. I feel my mother in particular gave us a much greater gift: the determination to work toward a goal. When Dad's salary was cut by two-fifths, he thought college was impossible for his three children. However, Mother, who had always wished that she had had more than just one year of college, was determined that we should graduate from college. She expected us to get good enough grades in high school for a scholarship, and we did not disappoint her.

Months before college started, she began suggesting job possibilities for us. We managed to earn most of our board bill. Mother and Dad were able to help us enough that we had time for some of the fun of college, too, but the major responsibility was up to us. I found that most of the people I admired were also helping to pay their way through college.

One real problem with the smaller families of this ecological age is that children will be overprotected and overindulged. The Christian family needs to develop an active concern in helping less fortunate families throughout the world. We can vouch for the satisfaction our family has had in looking after a boy in Korea through the Christian Children's Fund and helping two girls in France through Save the Children Federation.

The habit of sharing is important. Our children sometimes omitted dessert one night a week and put the money in a box designated for some specific charity. We have tried to stress that millions of people throughout the world go to bed hungry, and that it is selfish to buy such expensive foods that we don't have money left to share with others. Sharing does not come naturally to a child. It can come only through training, experience and time. If there are no other children in the family, then the wise parent sees that some are invited to the home so that the child learns to share.

Perhaps the present food shortages and high costs will teach Americans not to waste. Any schoolteacher can recount problems of getting children to eat their lunches. Mothers need to learn to use leftovers intelligently instead of throwing them down the garbage disposal.

There are still plenty of jobs for children to do in this automated world. Dishes don't fly from the dining room table to be washed or to be neatly stacked in the dishwasher. Tables don't set themselves, and dishes don't put themselves away. Waste paper has to be emptied and pets fed. Leaves need to be raked and lawns cut. For more creative tasks for children, try flower arrangements and looking after indoor plants.

When a child is little, it's far easier to do dishes or vacuum or make a cake without "help," but it isn't good for the child. If children haven't been trained from babyhood to help and to take their share of responsibility, they'll never learn it as teenagers. "Train up a child in the way he should go," the Book of Proverbs tells us. That applies to good behavior patterns such as learning to cooperate and to carry responsibility just as much as it applies to Biblical morality and the doctrines of the Church. If we wait until childhood is past to cultivate such things, we will have waited too long.

Many problems with teenagers come because children have never learned the value of money. Everything they ask for is given them. Each of our children was given an allowance for work performed, and with that he was expected to buy presents, pay club dues, give his Sunday school offering and provide for personal fun. When our three oldest children were 8, 11, and 12, they did their work well enough that they were hired for odd jobs by the neighbors.

I don't want my children to have *every advantage*. I believe that if more emphasis is put on sharing, responsibility and self-reliance, we will have fewer juvenile delinquents and a better world.

4

Does Your Husband Have a Place in Your Life?

WE WERE HAVING A STIMULATING DISCUSSION about child training. Each person in the group had a different theory and was expounding it vigorously.

Suddenly Dorothea spoke up. "I think happy parents are important, too. If children are to be secure, they need parents who are in love and take time for each other."

We agreed with Dorothea, and I thought of how well she exemplified what she had said. She and Tom were always full of ideas they wanted to discuss with each other. To go anywhere with them was a pleasure because they were such interesting conversationalists and obviously enjoyed each other's company. Although they had three children, once or twice a year Dorothea managed to leave the children with grandparents and go with Tom on a business trip to San Diego or San Francisco. They had as much fun together as newlyweds.

In those years my husband and I always envied Dorothea and Tom's trips together, but we thought that five children were too much to wish on anyone who wasn't accustomed to them. However, one spring I looked so tired after the children had been through a siege of measles and chicken pox that my mother volunteered to look after the children while my husband and I took a trip to San Francisco.

I had never been there before, and my husband took pride in showing me favorite spots and planning side trips to Monterey and Carmel. The trip was even nicer and more exciting than our first honeymoon, because newlyweds do not realize what a luxury it is to be alone. We came home, resolving to have at least one weekend trip alone each year, even if we had to topple the budget.

We feel that many divorces are the result of husband and wife taking each other for granted and failing to observe the little courtesies or to plan time for each other as they did when they were courting. We think of the happiest couples we know, and although many of them are busy people, they always manage to save time for each other and to make each minute count. A marriage in which each partner plans for some getting-together-alone time will always be zestful.

Meetings are not easy for my husband and me to avoid. He is very active in school and church affairs, and besides, he has a natural affinity for meetings.

We have given serious consideration to this activity so that meetings will serve to bring us closer together instead of pulling us apart. We refuse to schedule any meetings for weekends; we reserve this time for parties, family outings and family guests.

Every evening shortly before bedtime we take time out for tea and cookies. (In recent years I've had to omit the cookies.) As we have our refreshments, we talk over the happenings of the day. If Irving has been to a meeting, he reviews the highlights. In turn, I share with him my reading, my progress in writing, hobbies, and interesting family information.

These intimate talk-times also give us an opportunity to discuss with each other how we are feeling about our spiritual lives. If we are feeling down or are worried about anything, we can share it, pray about it, and plan a course of action that seems to both of us what God would want us to do.

Marriage counselors say that an engaged couple has a better chance for married happiness if their parents are happy and demonstrative toward one another. I first began to take Irving seriously after I had been invited to have dinner with his parents. Seeing their affectionate regard for each other, I thought, "If I can be that much in love after I've been married forty years, I'll have no complaints with my life."

My parents had very strict ideas of how my sister and I should behave on dates, but Mother was able to put her ideas over better than most parents because she always said, "Marriage is worth waiting for. A husband appreciates it if you save your affection for him." And seeing the sort of happy marriage Mother had managed for herself, Dot and I decided Mother couldn't be far wrong. Dad and Mother loved doing things together and were very demonstrative. Dad delighted in buying Mother beautiful lingerie and jewelry up to the time of his death.

Each couple can find different ways to show regard for each other. How they show it matters much less than the fact that they do show it. Any wife who shows her husband by her actions and attitudes that he is essential to her happiness will keep romance alive. Many a marriage could be lifted out of the doldrums if a husband and wife paid a little flattering attention to each other. A side benefit: you are helping your children when you have a happy marriage. Happy marriages tend to come to those who had happy parents.

5

What's the Gimmick?

IN A COURSE IN SHORT STORY WRITING we were told that frequently the gimmick helps sell the story. After all, the basic plots are repeated over and over again, but if a writer can give the plot a slightly different twist, his story may attract attention.

The same is true in real life. There are routine things that must be done and said in everyday living. Sometimes the parent can make the routine or the discipline more palatable by a gimmick.

One family was having frequent arguments because the teenage daughter wanted to have later hours on the weekend, but the parents were getting cross from losing their sleep while waiting up for her. Finally they hit upon a solution. Before parties, shows, etc., they decided upon a reasonable time for the daughter to be home (usually a compromise between the parents' and the daughter's ideas) and an alarm was set for 15 minutes past that time (allowing for red lights and other delays). The alarm was put outside the parents' door. If the daughter got home on time, she turned off the alarm and the parents' sleep was uninterrupted. If the daughter did not return on time, the alarm went off, the parents would wake up and begin to worry, and the daughter could count on losing some privileges.

My mother objected violently to arguing and fussing. Whenever we children argued, she would separate us and make us find something "nice" to say about the other person; for, as she explained, "Every person has virtues as well as faults." Often when I was stubborn and could not find anything complimentary to say about my sister except "Dot has a nice sister," that would start me laughing, and the quarrel would be forgotten.

Frequently a child misbehaves because he is tired and tense, and he simply needs isolation for a while. In those instances, we would put a child in his room and say, "You're not pleasant company right now. You need to stay in your room until you're ready to be with people."

Sometimes depriving a child of something he enjoys is effective, but often rewards produce more results than punishment or deprivation. I know there is a school of thought, particularly in pedagogy, which says, "Good behavior is its own reward. Don't encourage a child to seek false values." However, this school of thought does not take human nature into account. Even adults usually do better with praise than blame. Despite teachers who say good grades, etc., are an unrealistic system of rewards, both children and adults are stimulated by rewards.

During the summer my husband has often sold encyclopedias. Actually, since we needed the money to live on, the commission on each set sold should have been enough, but my husband always made the most sales when there was some sort of contest and he could accumulate points for a special prize, something more exciting than just paying the bills.

He gradually came to accept the fact that the same sort of incentive would inspire our children. In a yard as big as ours, there are a lot of leaves to rake. When he fussed and prodded the children, the work went slowly; but when I produced a sack of candy and he promised a piece for every basket of leaves picked up, it was amazing how fast the work went. Like other gimmicks, the reward gimmick should not be overused; a child should not expect a reward every time he behaves.

One mother found she saved arguments and recriminations and the family had a good laugh if she wrote her suggestions rather than saying them. Her teenage girl came home to find written in dust on her dresser, "Please clean this." The boy found this penciled jingle by the heaped-up clothes on his bed:

> You make your mother see red
> When you pile your clothes on your bed,
> If you want to bless 'er
> Put them in your dresser.

These gimmicks should vary from time to time if they are to keep their effectiveness. Just as no one would enjoy reading short stories if every author used the same gimmick, neither does a child keep on his toes with the same techniques used all the time. Sometimes we have used a "fine" drawer for clothes, books, etc., left in the wrong places. As I have cleaned, I have simply gone around with a box, collected all the things that were where they didn't belong, and dumped them in an extra drawer in the kitchen. Dad was charged double what the children were to redeem his articles because his allowance was bigger, and often people were glad to pay money to redeem things because they couldn't remember where they had left them. At other times a bulletin board on the back porch has reminded people of duties and schedules. The cleverest mothers I know always include some new cartoons on the bulletin board so that people look at it regularly.

Sickness can sometimes be as strenuous for the mother as for the patient. One of the difficulties, unless two are sick at the same time, is boredom or lack of anticipation. A number of inexpensive packages attractively wrapped, some even of forgotten toys, might be put in a big box. The child then sets the alarm for the time he can open a package, perhaps one an hour, and during the time in between he can play with the contents of the package just opened.

Different gimmicks need to be used with teen-agers, particularly gimmicks that develop their sense of independence and initiative. At times I complained that as soon as our children got fairly good at a job, the neighbors hired them out from under me. However, I really was thankful for the training the neighbors gave them. If I tried to show them a better or more efficient way of doing things, I was nagging or fussy, but if the neighbor who was paying them so much an hour showed them a different way, she was "clever," and her suggestions were accepted and brought home to me.

In addition, neighbors can often uncover hidden talents. I had never thought our youngest daughter efficient or persistent enough to paint. She worked for a neighbor who was expecting her third child and yet wanted her house sparkling fresh when in-laws came to visit. When I stopped to see the neighbor, I was astounded to discover that my youngest son had washed all her walls, and that our youngest daughter had painted the kitchen, a difficult two-color job, done more neatly than I could have done it.

Occasionally teenagers can get to fussing and clowning and slamming each other so that it is miserable to be around them. This is especially true on a long trip when you are together most of your waking hours. Rather than nagging, we hit on this procedure: "This trip is using up our savings. You're no addition when you act this way. If we have to speak again, you pay for the next meal." There is no reason, in this day when teenagers are able to earn and save, that they should not contribute something, particularly if they are not contributing good humor at the moment.

41

Often teenagers can learn about the difficulties in a situation when they are permitted to take over, and they become more understanding of the problems adults face. The drivers of the family were often critical of my husband's driving (and I'll admit that although it is expert, it is too relaxed for European traffic and roads). My husband had Dave take over the driving, and as Dave discovered the difficulties of finding parking places, of one-way streets, etc., he insisted that his dad do his half of the driving.

Whether gimmicks or creative strategies, call them what you will, imaginative approaches to child guidance and discipline will lead to happier days.

6

Why Not Use Camp Techniques in the Home?

DOES IT SEEM AS IF you spend half of your time saying, "Johnny, you didn't wash your ears"; "Jimmy, have you brushed your teeth?" and "Mary, your room's a mess"? Do you repeat each request about five times and then finally have to get cross to be obeyed?

Visit a boys' camp for a day and see how discipline and routine are managed. The techniques used are admirably fitted to a regular family. With 50 to 60 boys in camp, no counselor has time to make the same request five times. With the vigorous activities of horseback riding, swimming, archery, and riflery going on simultaneously, boys must obey safety rules or miss out on the fun.

Although each camp has mature men on its staff, much of the work and counseling are done by older high school boys and college fellows. Yet these fellows often manage the boys more easily than their own parents can, and camps have fewer accidents than most homes. What is the secret?

I'd say the answer lies in only a few words:

43

routine, contests, and a few rules strictly enforced.

Do you waste thousands of words a day about cleanliness and neatness? Rivalry between two different camp groups—Apaches or Mohicans, Sioux or Navahos—helps to take care of this difficult problem. Shortly after breakfast comes tent inspection. Each tribe strives for a 100 percent record. Every boy is checked for brushed teeth, clean ears, clean hands and face, clean socks and a neat bedroll and tent. Points are deducted for anyone who is not up to a standard. Each week the winning team is given a special treat: a watermelon feed, an excursion, or an extra dessert.

Some sort of rivalry often is necessary to get the sloths moving during summer vacation. Each person can represent an Indian tribe, a TV hero, or whatever happens to be the current interest of your children. Or you could keep charts for the individual child, and give special treats for superior charts. Occasionally, you might pit the boys in the family against the girls, but that should not be the most frequent arrangement. We do not want to imply to our children that competitiveness is the primary relationship between the sexes.

A mother could save her tongue a lot of exercise if rooms and the appearance of the children were ready for inspection before the children left for play in summer or school during the year. Let Dad be camp director. Takes too much time? Isn't this method quicker than searching for books, homework, rain gear, etc., at the last moment? Or discovering on the morning you entertain your church circle that not a bed is made, and you have to make them yourself or suffer the reputation of a poor housekeeper?

A good camp director sets up a routine that is easy to follow and that will eliminate most points of discipline and trouble. For example, unplanned meals can cause a dither of confusion. At camp, before each meal, two bells are rung—one as a warning to wash and the last as a signal to come to the Chuck Shack. Before anyone may enter the Shack, the counselor must OK the clean appearance of each Indian. Dishes must be stacked and cleared before any group is excused.

In camp, showers must be taken on certain days, letters written home, etc. Arguments will be avoided if no exceptions are made to routine. Bedtime comes at a regular time, and talking is discouraged. Do you have a general routine to follow and are you fairly consistent in your standards so that your child knows what is expected of him?

Camp rules are few and are aimed at the children's safety and welfare. Boys who persistently disobey rules are deprived of privileges or even sent away from camp. For example, although boys may run all they want uphill, no one is permitted to run downhill. Too many accidents happen that way. For archery and riflery, boys must stand back of a certain mark while shooting, or they lose those sports. For swimming the boy must not only obey safety rules, but he must put his clothes in a neat pile on the beach before he can go in the water.

45

Untidiness reflects on the camp, and boys are taught to take pride in the camp's good name. Does your child feel a responsibility for maintaining the family's good name?

No sloths in camp. Every boy is expected to take his turn washing dishes, raking, building the fire or hanging up the newly washed clothes. The lazy ones who fall down on the job are ostracized or given the more disagreeable jobs, like cleaning the site of outdoor plumbing.

In a good camp routine, the contests, a few rules definitely enforced, and group pride and spirit help to keep discipline problems to a minimum. A little planning and imagination at home can help to eliminate most discipline problems.

7

Do Your Children Work for You?

I THOUGHT I COULD HEAR the jingle of the telephone over the vacuum cleaner. When I rushed to answer the phone, I heard Sharon's voice.

"Why aren't you on your way home?" I demanded. "You're supposed to clean your room before company gets here for dinner."

"My teacher needs me," pleaded Sharon. "She has so much to do toward the end of school. Please, can't I stay to help her clean out the cupboards?"

"All right," I agreed, "but only for half an hour. I need you at home."

It was then that I decided something should be done to make work at home as interesting as it was away from home. Our children had always helped around the house. Five children of stair-step ages had to be trained to do their jobs if the family was to have time for fun. Now I was losing my workers because neighbors and teachers were asking for their help.

During that summer vacation, both Marilynne

47

and Sharon had jobs helping neighbors with housework. Our two oldest children were kept so busy with baby-sitting and housekeeping jobs for the neighbors that they couldn't get excited over doing any more for our house than they had to.

I liked having the girls earn money. It was good training, and they made good use of the money they earned. But they were losing interest in working around the home, and the younger children were following their example.

How could I make helping me interesting for all our children? At that time I couldn't afford to pay them as the neighbors did, for a schoolteacher's salary is at its lowest ebb during summer months.

What was the fascination of working for other people? After all, Sharon's teacher didn't pay her. I was once a schoolteacher, too, and my students were good about helping me, not just for apple-polishing either. What could we parents learn from the teachers and employers?

First, they were appreciative. Parents are too prone to take work as their due and be more generous with correction than with praise. One neighbor, Jane, was allergic to cleaning aids. She kept telling the girls how wonderful they were to help her so that her hands didn't get sore. The other neighbor had an invalid mother-in-law. She told Marilynne how her help gave her more time. The teachers praised the children for being good workers.

In addition to the use of praise, both teachers and employers are likely to set up more definite guidelines than parents do, and they require the children to follow them. I had nagged for years about wiping off the sink, cleaning the stove and leaving the kitchen neat, but after working at Jane's, Marilynne said, "We must keep our kitchen cleaner. It would never pass Jane's inspection." Jane had a checklist of jobs that had to be completed before dishes were considered done: clean stove and refrigerator, wipe off sink, wipe off cupboards, put away dishes, put away supplies.

Finally, the employers had good equipment. Because they were paying by the hour, they bought the soap the girls preferred and kept on hand the easiest forms of silver polishes, window cleaners and waxes. I was likely to use makeshift supplies that cost less.

The teachers used the incentive of status in school; the employers offered wages and pleasant working conditions. What could I offer?

Suddenly it came to me. All our children are sociable. They love company and good times. They like parties and friends staying overnight. I like company, too, but there's no denying that company makes extra work, and I was reluctant to promise the parties they wanted. Our summer was already busy, for a neighbor with a swimming pool had invited the children to swim every day that I could come with them to swim and supervise. I love swimming, but a big house, community and church responsibilities, and five children did not leave much time for swimming.

We had an informal family council to plan how

we could have more time for swimming and entertaining, and came up with a chart of extra jobs. Each child (at that time ages 5, 7, 9, 11, 13) was expected to make his own bed. The four oldest worked on dishes and wastepaper. They also did yardwork regularly. But there were a number of extra jobs they could do that would considerably lighten my load if they were given enough incentive to make the work fun.

A chart emerged with these rewards. The two youngest were expected to do one half hour's extra work each week to earn the right to go swimming. The oldest were expected to do two hours of extra work for that privilege. Other extra work rewards were:

1 hour earns a guest for the afternoon and refreshments.

2 hours of extra work earn a guest for a meal.

5 hours earn one overnight guest.

10 hours earn two overnight guests.

15 hours earn a party with refreshments.

20 hours earn a party with a meal, such as hamburgers, tacos, waffles or spaghetti.

Each family naturally would have a different list of jobs to earn company. This was our list:

1. yardwork: cutting lawn, extra raking of leaves, weeding, clipping off dead branches
2. mending and darning
3. washing and ironing
4. polishing silver
5. scrubbing floors
6. cleaning out drawers

7. cleaning up play areas
8. practicing reading or piano or times tables
9. making skirts, pajamas, blouses; careful work on Christmas presents
10. making cookies, cake
11. making powdered milk
12. cleaning stove or refrigerator
13. cleaning sink or washing cupboards
14. helping to clean basement or garage
15. taking care of bird
16. listening to Kathleen read
17. reading to Robert
18. fixing a meal
19. washing dishes at dinner
20. helping with canning
21. waxing floors
22. waxing furniture

We decided that for the older children not more than one-third of the time could be earned on personal projects, or Sharon would try to earn all of hers with piano practice.

After the project had been in use for a while, I asked the children their opinion. Verdicts ranged from "swell" to "super wonderful" from Marilynne who had given a hamburger bake that was so popular that her friends had been urging her to repeat the party. Her status as a teenager was definitely raised.

The children were thinking of the fun they had entertaining, but I also noticed the difference in their attitudes toward their work.

With this system they looked for jobs instead of

trying to avoid them. They felt important keeping their own records and earning the right to entertain more. A great deal of nagging was eliminated, both in regard to extra jobs and their regular work. Rooms were inspected at 9:15 in the morning during summer and before bedtime when school was on. Clean rooms earned a 15-minute bonus each time; dirty rooms subtracted 15 minutes; and so-so rooms kept the points the same.

Parties and entertaining may not be as important for your children. They may have another goal in mind. One friend had a daughter who loved new clothes. When illness in the family made it necessary for her to hire help, her 13-year-old daughter asked for the job. She used the money she earned for clothes and to save toward college. Our girls had paying jobs and needed other stimuli.

Another friend comes from a background of army tradition. She had her oldest daughter organize the work of a group of youngsters when they came for a beach weekend. Rank was earned by the amount of work that was done, and the mother hostess found she had nothing to do. After all, no one wanted to be a private; everyone was working to be a general. All that is needed is a little imagination to make work have value. Work achieves meaning and purpose when it helps adults or children toward a goal.

For us, the system of fun rewards worked. I enjoyed my shining windows which the girls volunteered to wash. It was wonderful having the younger children make a conscious effort to keep their rooms clean. I liked happy groups of youngsters around the house now that I had the time for them. And Marilynne and Sharon, excitedly phoning boys and girls to a Come-as-You-Are party, believed the system gave them their hearts' desire.

8

Reevaluating Techniques
for Today's World

MANY PEOPLE ARE NOT FINDING JOY through their children and family life as they should because they are worrying too much about the moral environment in which their children are growing up. I can understand parental concern. I've had it, too. I know that people are affected by the standards of those around them. The sexual permissiveness of the time, the pornography, the drug scene, the crime and violence, the riots—all these things can lead to worry for any parent.

In the last ten years people seem to have been catapulted into change whether they wanted it or not. There are not quite eight years between our oldest and our youngest children, and yet the differences occurring in society in those eight years are unbelievable. When Marilynne and Sharon went to the University of Redlands there were strict regulations in the dormitory about hours, and where the boys could be. Regulations were also firm at state schools. College students were concerned about integration and peace. When our youngest son started to U.C.L.A. in 1969, there were no rules in the dormitories at all. Although supposedly girls had one side of the dorm and boys the other, girls were wandering up and down the halls and into the boys' rooms at all times of the day and night. Stereos were blaring continually. Students who were serious about their studying got apartments because the dorms were never quiet.

In spite of all this, need parents be so worried? True, it is a time of ferment and change, but not all change is for the worse. There are as many hopeful signs as there are discouraging ones. The young people of today who are interested in church seem to have deeper interests than those which characterized the social punch-and-cookies syndrome of the late fifties.

Recently when our minister started an evening Bible study on Romans, many high school and college people joined the study group, along with the middle-aged and elderly. This year the young people of our church decided to give up part of their Christmas vacation to work at the church camp with a group of the mentally and physically handicapped who are part of a sheltered work project.

It's been a long time since I've seen such concern for the world, such interest in the Bible, such depth of Christian feeling as I have seen among young people today. We are in a time of crisis, and the world could go either way. The Chinese characters for *crisis* signify both *danger* and *opportunity,* words that describe our time. How meaningful to be a parent now and to emphasize the word *opportunity!*

At a recent conference of church workers, Dr. Don Locher of Santa Barbara preached a sermon on Psalm 137. He emphasized that in a new land, we need to be willing to sing a new song, as the Jews did by the waters of Babylon, but that the new song must have the old truths in it. He applied the psalm particularly to parents and workers with youth. It doesn't matter whether we worship God with guitars or with the organ. God loves people with long hair as well as people with short hair. But we can't compromise the message. Church people are not made to conform to society, but to try to change the parts of society that are wrong. The Ten Commandments are still relevant. The Sermon on the Mount should challenge us in our living. In times of danger and confusion and conflicting values, we must be willing to sacrifice for what we believe.

Probably there is no more important thing we can teach our children than the idea that they should do what is right, regardless of what others do. In recent years many people have tended to go along with the crowd under the misguided idea that we have a Christian, educated democracy, and whatever the majority chooses is right. That is not what the apostle Paul taught in Romans 12: 2. He decried conformity to worldly standards. J. B. Phillips paraphrased this verse marvelously. He wrote it: "Don't let the world around you squeeze you into its own mold, but let God remold your minds from within, so that you may prove in practice that the plan of God for you is good, meets all his demands and moves toward the goal of true maturity."

Young people have always been challenged by idealism. Even the violence of the late sixties and early seventies was partly caused by young people who wanted changes for the better—right away—and saw violence as a viable option. Many of them now have learned that they cannot use violence for good ends; the means determine the ends. Some of these young people are realizing that the way of God is the way to change the world. How exciting to be alive now and to be a parent, helping your children find a new world through God!

9

The First Baby

THE WAY YOUNG PARENTS start the training of a
first baby may determine whether they will want
any more. A baby can be a joy that adds glow to
everyday life or he can be a whining tyrant who
begins his domination of his parents with crying
and finishes it with whining, complaining, griping,
and saying, "Everybody else does it." Ideally
young parents should have the time to give their
child love and attention, and yet have enough
major concerns that the baby learns to adapt his
schedule to group welfare.

When I was expecting our first baby, I was overwhelmed with the schedules that the so-called experts set up. To fulfill them, I would have had to
neglect my husband; and with the war on and Irving working as a conscientious objector in forestry
camps, Indian service, and a mental hospital, it was
necessary for me to earn the living. Consequently,
I simplified the schedules considerably. Any good
baby book can give the essential information on
health and child care. I had read Dr. Arnold

Gesell's book, *The First Five Years of Life,* and we owned the *Better Homes and Gardens Baby Book* and Dr. Spock's book.

The important thing, though, is the attitude parents develop. A baby needs love and a certain amount of attention, but he is also part of the human race and has responsibilities. The world does not revolve around him.

Let me first recommend breast-feeding, if it is at all possible. It is cheaper, more convenient, saves time, improves the mother's health, and forces her to take time for the baby. All five of our children were breast-fed, varying from five months to almost a year, and they have been extremely healthy. It forced me to sit down and relax at least every four hours; and it gave me time to play with her (or him) and also time to catch up with my reading, a factor important to my mental and spiritual health. Because I worked eight hours a day when the first two were babies, they learned to take a bottle for the middle feeding.

Because of our lack of time and money, and due to gasoline rationing, our children learned to sleep in their buggies anywhere we took them. They were kept clean and warm and fed at regular intervals, but were never permitted extreme "demand" feeding either as babies or preschoolers. They were expected to eat at mealtimes, with one midmorning and one midafternoon snack, but they were not permitted to nibble all day long. If there was no reason for a baby's crying and he continued to cry, he was isolated. He did not get picked up by crying. However, since our children liked to be with people when they were awake and happy, they were usually in a playpen or bassinet or on a blanket nearby when we worked at home.

Toddlers have a right to be read to before naps and bed and to enjoy adult company, as long as they behave. However, a child who is loved and given proper attention should not be permitted to dominate an adult gathering or to interrupt adults constantly as they are talking. Toddlers need friends their own age, and so do their parents. A mother who wants to enjoy her family needs to train her baby or toddler to adjust to other people's routines and rights. My philosophy evolved because it was necessary for me to earn the living when our first two were babies; and by the time our third was on the way and I quit work, there was so much to do that I didn't have time to give any of my children an excess of attention. I discovered they were nice in spite of a busy mother.

Now a report in the December 17, 1971, *Life* tells me I used the wrong phrase; it was not "in spite of a busy mother" but "because of." The Harvard Pre-School Project was set up to discover why some children seem to have a built-in handicap when they start school; others seem bound to succeed. Dr. Burton L. White and his associates discovered that although home backgrounds seem similar, Group "A" children rated exceptional in all areas, not just reading, whereas Group "C" seemed unable to cope. As they began to research the children's early years, they found that the time from 10 to 18 months was most vital in determining whether a child would be in the "A" group or the "C" group. The researchers observed the mothers of 40 children of this age group, an age at which the child begins to get into everything.

Astonishingly enough, they discovered the "A" mothers seldom gave their child undivided attention. They kept poisons and sharp utensils out of reach, but otherwise the children were given some freedom to explore and were not constantly confined to a playpen or a high chair. When the child brings her something he's discovered, the mother may take only 20 seconds, but she shows interest and excitement. She encourages him to master some jobs himself. Because she is busy, sometimes even with a part-time job, she utilizes changing diapers and routine tasks to express love or a sense of fun.

The "C" mother tends to be overprotective, both of the child and of her home. She restricts her child's tendency to explore, seldom encouraging her baby's attempts at making sense of the world. A neighbor began remodeling her house about the time her boy started the toddler stage. I marveled at the way her boy stayed in his playpen, whereas our Dave, who was about the same age, was into everything. Finally, when her boy was about three he emerged from his playpen cocoon, and he's been into trouble ever since. Actually, the description of the "C" mother more often fits the mother of one or two children who refuses to do anything for others.

My philosophy had a touch of selfishness in it; as a mother I still wanted time for my husband and for my hobbies. Now I discover science justifies me.

10

Keep Your Eye Upon the Doughnut

"OH, BROTHER!" I exclaimed impatiently. I had just turned my head for a moment, and Bobby had toppled his milk. Then, as I was mopping up the mess, I really *saw* the breakfast room floor. I had been so busy trying to get the washing out and the beds changed that I hadn't swept the room after breakfast. There were Cheerios and cornflakes by David and Marilynne's chairs, and suddenly I discovered what had happened to the toast Kathleen was supposed to have finished. Sharon had sugar underneath her chair. David had been cutting pictures from breakfast food cartoons, and scraps were all over the floor.

As I lifted my head, I saw what Kathleen had done while I was cleaning up Bobby's mess. "Kathleen Garrison," I threatened, "next time we have tomato soup, you'll wear your plastic bib, regardless of how much you like that cloth one. It's no better than a sieve when you spill soup all down you."

Gloomily I hurried the three children through

their meal and put the two youngest down for their naps. It had been one of "those" days. There had been such a high fog that I was sure it would rain, so I'd tried to hang all but the big things down in the basement, but there just wasn't room. I thought of friends who put off their washings when Monday was unpleasant, but they either had fewer than five children or automatic washers and driers, or perhaps more changes of underwear and socks.

I decided to wallow in self-pity. I put water on for tea and went to look for the mail. A letter from Bob, my brother in Korea! I luxuriously sat down with tea, cookies, and the mail. In my last letter to Bob I had asked him if he ever became discouraged and disillusioned by the misery, brutality, and poverty that he saw. This was his reply:

War is terrible, Marge, but we see some fine, heroic things too. Do you remember that picture that hung in the wall in Mother's breakfast room? A jolly fat man sat eating a doughnut that was all doughnut, while nearby was a mournful skeleton with a doughnut that was all hole. I can still say the rhyme on the picture, and when I'm looking on the gloomy side, I repeat to myself:

As you ramble on through life, brother,
Whatever be your goal,
Keep your eye upon the doughnut
And not upon the hole.

With a guilty start I thought, "Why, that applies

to me!" How many times had I said longingly, "When the children are older, maybe I'll have time to do more things"? Or, "When the children are all in school, maybe the house will stay clean"? When the children were all in school perhaps the house would stay clean and I would have more time for my hobbies and doing my share in community enterprises, but there would be so much that I would miss. It would be lonesome without a baby around the house. Babies are such adorably cuddly creatures. (I feel the same way now that I have grandchildren. I could start all over again!)

I remembered when I had been a school librarian, trying to catalog books, rearrange shelves, order new books, with the constant interruptions of students asking for help or causing some disturbance. The three weeks' work alone in the library after school was closed gave me plenty of time for uninterrupted work, but they also brought boring monotony and a feeling of no immediate need. No one could say that life with five children, three not yet in school, was monotonous. They also made me feel useful and definitely needed.

After the children were in bed that night, I recalled the old motto to my husband.

"It's corny," Irving commented, "but maybe you've got something at that. We really do have a big doughnut in our lives."

As the days passed I began to count the ingredients that made up my doughnut, or the doughnut of any parents of small children. The hole was always there—dirt, noise, and constant work—but the doughnut was seeming bigger and bigger.

It seemed very big when I got a letter from Louise who had had another miscarriage. Louise had married only a few months after I did and loved children, but she had none. She wrote sadly that she might as well begin putting her name in at the adoption agencies. Children may forget to hang up clothes, scatter paper over the floor (Kathleen was at the cutting stage) and leave dirty tracks over freshly scrubbed kitchen floors, but how empty life would be without them! When I thought of the many people who longed for children and my own richness in having five, I felt singularly blessed.

A few minutes earlier, when I was staring at the mess on the breakfast-room floor, I could not have smiled at the psalmist's comparison of children to a warrier's arrows (Psalm 127) and the verse that says, "Happy is the man who has his quiver full of them!" Now I could. The exasperation of the moment was over, and my perspective was all right again.

A few days later I had a moment of glee at the ease with which I turned down a PTA job I didn't want. I had only to say, "I couldn't possibly take it. Besides the two children at school I have three at home, ages one, three, and almost five." There was a gasp over the phone from Mrs. Williams and the apologetic, "Oh, I didn't know. Of course, you can't do it."

I managed time to be a Blue Bird leader and to

do the jobs I actually enjoy most, but it was handy to have a never-questioned excuse for the jobs that didn't particularly interest me and that took me away from home during the day.

As the days went by I began to be less concerned about the dirt and noise, and hugged to my heart the dear memories. Language could not capture the singing joy that came to me as I noticed our children in interesting stages. I thought, "Words make the pictures seem so prosaic, but all parents must treasure these precious moments."

I thought of some of those moments—Bobby's curly head resting against my shoulder when I picked him up; Kathleen imitating the big girls and getting very dramatic about the antics of her doll; Kathleen flirting with her daddy; David, suddenly growing up and helping clear the table and empty the wastepaper baskets so he would be big enough to go to kindergarten the next fall; Marilynne and Sharon reading to the younger children and taking them on buggy rides; Kathleen cuddling Smokey, her little gray kitty; Bobby, trying to talk and managing a "thank oo" for everything; Bobby, flopping like a fish in his bath. I decided that even though they meant more work, these precious days when the children were learning so much must not slide dully by, but must be enjoyed to the fullest.

I saw in our young children the chance to instill a foundation for a growing love for God. I could help them know that God loves each of them and us as a family. This was my time to build into them a positive response to the church by showing how much we valued our involvement with its programs and people. I also realized that this was the time to communicate my ideals, and to help our children understand that these ideals grow out of my faith in God.

I rejoiced at the unprejudiced way the children formed their friendships. When Sharon and Marilynne asked to bring children home from school, I seldom knew until they arrived what race they would be. I felt I could forget nonessentials like untied shoelaces, clothes under the bed, and water on the floor when Sharon said one day, "It would be fun if we had different neighbors."

"What do you mean?" I asked. "I think our neighbors are lovely."

"So do I," agreed Sharon, "but it would be fun to have a Japanese girl my age next door, and a black girl, and an Indian and some children from the countries in Europe. I'd like to have all kinds of friends to play with every day."

"Why do adults lose their sense of wonder and enjoyment of life?" I asked myself another day as David came running in and asked me to look at the new flower that was putting up shoots. David made a regular ritual of inspecting the yard every day and noticing each change, but I often became too involved and concerned about work and trivialities. "We have this nice home and yard and I seldom take time just to enjoy them the way David does," I thought.

There were still times when the children were young that I longed for quiet and cleanliness and a house that always looked like an illustration for a beautiful-home magazine, but more and more as I counted up the ingredients that went into my life's doughnut, I discovered that I was enjoying my doughnut too much to notice the hole.

11

First Things First

Trust a pair of schoolteachers to think of the primary years as being extremely important in determining whether a child will make a success of his life. It is then that a child learns the basic skills he will need all his life: reading and arithmetic, learning to work with others and adjusting to rules and regulations. If these skills are not mastered, the child will have trouble with schoolwork and authority all of his life. In spite of the use of films, tapes and TV, most basic learning is conveyed through reading, and if a child does not learn to read well, he will have trouble both in school and in amusing himself.

What can a parent do to help? If nothing else, the Head Start program has proved that parents who do not give their children a cultural background handicap them from the start. A parent who wants his child to enjoy reading must enjoy reading himself. There should be books, magazines and music in the house. From the time our children could say a few words, I began to read picture books to them and later more difficult books. Having a book to read was a part of the nap or bedtime routine. This procedure not only makes school appealing; it makes the bed routine easier.

Picnics, drives, beach and mountain trips, and visits to the zoo help a child to know what words like *cow, ocean, mountains, waves, hay, monkey* and *elephant* mean. A child with a rich background learns more easily.

Bible story books certainly ought to take their place among the other books parents provide for their children. An early awareness of God's love and care can be given to a child through the adventures of others who learned that God loved them and helped them.

Fortunately, publishers today are making a wide range of children's Bible story books available. Some have pop-up features that add interest; others come with accompanying phonograph records that take the child through the book page by page. Simplified versions of the Bible itself are available for children, including a picture-strip version that appeals especially to the middle and older child.

Just as parents' enthusiasm for reading in general cultivates in their children a warm response to learning by reading, an appreciation of God and the Bible and the church can be encouraged by providing good Christian reading material from early childhood onward.

I don't think children in a big family need the nursery school routine as much as children in families of one or two children. However, Sunday school gives a child experience in playing with other children, in sharing, in adjusting. I took our three younger children to preschool one morning a week, not so much because they needed the contact with other children, but because they wanted to copy their older sisters and go to school. In California, preschool is free and is listed under parent-education courses. All our three younger children had birthdays that made them start school later, and the last year before kindergarten they needed something like preschool to challenge them.

Marilynne was the only child to have three-hour kindergarten (before school funds were cut) and she had preprimer and beginning reading training, something that is available now only in private schools. As a result, all of our five children were started on preprimers in the summer between kindergarten and first grade. Every week we would go to the library and pick out books, starting with the easiest and building up to more difficult stories.

Some children pick up reading extremely quickly so that they are reading books like *Alice in Wonderland* by the second grade. Although some of our children don't read as fast as I think they should, all were in the fast-reading group in their primary classes and in the good to accelerated classes throughout school.

Reading is learned by practice, just as is typing or any other skill, and a teacher with 30 students in her class cannot give each child the individual practice he needs. ·Parents need to help if they want their children to read well. One note of warning. Love and praise should be used to develop this skill, not fussing and nagging. A parent must be patient. If a child is to enjoy reading, it must be associated with pleasant experiences.

A child can be preconditioned to math by games—counting with a ball, skill games and board games. We used to amuse ourselves while we were doing the dishes by reciting the times tables or arithmetic combinations. My husband, who hated arithmetic as a child and was the despair of his principal father, was amazed to hear us doing math for fun. My family has always been a games family, and you need to know math if you are to keep score; so our children have been exposed to math since they were about two-years-old. I also used flash cards during the summer reading period, and we would make a game over who could say the answer first and get to keep the card. (What hilarity when sometimes the youngest child won!)

The whole school and learning process, particularly through the first few years, should be made pleasant. Before school starts, a child should have training in safety and in crossing the street. At least a week before the first session, the mother or father should practice walking, taking the correct turns, etc., with the child so that he knows his way to school. As much as possible, after the first day, I think a child should walk to school by himself. He needs to learn independence and dependability. Ground rules should be set up about phoning if he stops at some friend's house.

Our three younger children had to walk or ride their bikes a long distance during most of their school years, and they learned to be independent and fend for themselves. A mother will spend most of her time walking or driving to and from school if children don't learn independence.

We always took some part in PTA, went to the school open houses and found time for parent conferences because we knew from the teacher's point of view how important these were. Each child during elementary school could invite his teacher (and family, if any) to dinner. The social affair made school seem important, and the children built up friendships that have lasted over the years. (Both Marilynne's second grade and fourth grade teachers came to her wedding.)

This was the time to enlarge our children's horizons from home and church to the school and the community. This was the time to begin Blue Birds, Brownies and Indian Guides. This was the time we went to the "Y's" monthly family potlucks and swims. This was the time we had families over for backyard barbecues and games of darts and croquet. The primary years are important years in getting a child interested in school and in his community.

77

12

Hi, Juniors!

To me the junior age is the easiest age of all, and I know it is for my husband. That's why he has remained a fifth or sixth-grade teacher rather than going into administration or secondary teaching as so many men do.

Not that there isn't drama and difficulty in this age. It is the time for broken arms and legs, for skinned knees and torn blue jeans, for measles and chicken pox. But it's an uncomplicated age. You can see progress, and children respond to understanding and suggestions. If a good foundation for discipline has been laid during the early years, routine spiced with gimmicks seems to answer the problems. You don't have to go through a traumatic experience each time to enforce discipline, as you may in the two-year-old or teenage stage. This is the time when the family is a close-knit unit and children enjoy family picnics and outings; they want their parents to take part in PTA and Camp Fire Girls. Organized church activities, such as children's choir or vacation Bible school or boys' and girls' camps, rate high enthusiasm.

Sports seem to go by seasons, with such subtle changes that no parent can seem to sense the difference. But no one would think of starting jacks until it's the time that everyone plays; suddenly it may be the time for hopscotch, or four score, or jump rope. The wind, of course, determines kite season, but baseball, basketball, and volleyball do not always follow the collegiate schedule.

If as an adult you still have any of these skills, you have achieved status. My husband had charge of the school physical education program for three or four years and can still hold his own. I haven't lost my skill with jacks or with Ping-Pong, so I still can provide exciting competition. One of my favorite aunts played jacks with her nieces.

This is the heyday of the clubs. If the juniors are not active in Blue Birds and Camp Fire Girls, Brownies and Girl Scouts, Indian Guides, Cub Scouts and Boy Scouts, they often have a secret neighborhood club or put out a neighborhood newspaper. Unless you are allergic to large groups of children, I would urge that a busy mother limit her outside civic efforts to this sort of group; the adult groups can always use your help later. It's such a short time that your children will want you to be important in their social activities. After the junior age, parent participation is often scorned.

This is the time to lay in a good supply of bandages, antiseptics and blue-jean patches if your children are at all adventurous. In fact, the escapades, diseases and torn clothes are the biggest hazards for parents at this age.

This also is the time to be sure that your child is doing well at school. Children develop at different rates of speed, and not all children are good readers at the end of the second or third grade. David's reading began to improve considerably in the fourth grade when he had a teacher who shared his gardening interest and concern about flowers, but who also insisted that with his IQ, he should be reading harder books and more books. His teacher's insistence and his grandfather's gift of a subscription to a children's book club pushed his reading skill to new levels.

If a child has not fairly well learned his basic three Rs by the time he is through the fifth grade, the parent needs to check with the teacher to see what she can do to help. Perhaps tutoring, special classes, or even a different type of school might fit his needs better. The sixth grade is the last year before the more departmentalized work of junior high and high school, and recently in some school areas, departmentalization has already started.

This is a time of interest in crafts and winning honors. Both Camp Fire and Cub Scouts use crafts in nearly all their meetings. There is a tremendous interest in passing rank that often loses momentum by the time the girls, at least, get into eighth and ninth grade. In school and in clubs children make presents for their fathers, mothers or other relatives. In Camp Fire we baked cookies, made fudge and divinity, and experimented with "s'mores" at camp-outs. We had booths of our crafts or our cooking at PTA carnivals. The boys built model airplanes or cars, and often every card table in the house was set up with an unfinished craft which could not be disturbed.

It's also a time for collections and scrapbooks. Nearly every child has a stamp or coin or even a matchbook collection of sorts. Sometimes a lifelong interest is begun, although often the collection doesn't survive junior high. David is the only one of our five who still as an adult spends time and money for stamps. Girls turn to scrapbooks, both for fun and for schoolwork, and often a fifth or sixth-grade teacher will receive a beautifully illustrated report.

With some children a lifelong hobby is started, but with many children the collection or the scrapbook is simply a phase of the junior age. I moved to California when I was nine, so I was fascinated by movie star pictures. Nothing could interest me less now. However, I still have my poetry scrapbooks, my recipes, my pictures of rooms and furniture I like. When I was a child, I used to say that if there were a fire the first thing I would rescue would be my scrapbooks. When we did have a fire at our cabin, the one thing of value David rescued was his stamp collection.

When a mother feels that she cannot stand for one minute more the mess and litter of collections, scrapbooks, and crafts, she needs to remember her own enthusiasm at this age. A house is made for the people in it, not the people for the house. And remember, there are benefits. Children of this age can play hours at a time, with far longer interest span than when they were tiny. At the junior age, it is no longer necessary to have a feeling of uneasiness if children are quiet for a long time. They are probably absorbed in a craft, not pouring furniture polish over a davenport or writing with crayon on the wallpaper.

Often this is the homeliest age for a child. There is no longer the baby softness and dimples; the teenage interest in clothes has not begun. It is as if God said to parents, "This is the age when you have the least worries. Enjoy it and don't ask for beauty too."

13

I'm Not Jealous of Teenagers

MY GIRLS' HAIR hung in lanky, damp strands.
Bothered that they did not look their best, I
ventured a suggestion. "How about a home permanent?"

The girls faced me with a stare of withering
scorn. "Oh, you adults are so critical of teenagers.
You're jealous of us."

I looked back at the girls in open-mouthed
amazement. I was too astounded to utter even a
word. Jealous of teenagers! Oh, no! Deliver me
from having to live again through the agonies of
adolescence. Deliver me from alternating again
between an adolescent's depths of despair and
heights of ecstasy. I thought myself so unjealous
that the accusation shocked me. But what stunned
me the most was that I was being classified as a
nonunderstanding and difficult adult.

During the time our five children were growing
up I had always ignored the magazine articles on
teenagers. My thinking turned on logic like this:
"Well, during nursery age or grammar-school age

children may at times baffle me, but at least I know teenagers."

Since I had taught high school students for five years, I was certain that I really knew young people. I had worked with teenagers on the school newspaper. I had coached them in dramatic productions. I had sponsored many school activities. A lot of teenagers had confided their at-home problems to me. Since my public school teaching days, I had kept up with teenagers by teaching in the high school department at Sunday school for a number of years. I thought I knew teenagers!

Clearly it was time for me to do some rethinking about teenagers. I needed to wonder why, for the past six months, our two teenagers had often been bored by the idea of family outings and hyper-critical of anyone who was not a teenager. Perhaps I was making some big mistakes in dealing with our teenagers. I began to remember my own teen years, and how I vowed then that I wouldn't show the lack of understanding I felt my own parents had.

Suddenly it dawned on me that what I had been telling other parents for years applied to me. If children are to grow up and cut the apron strings (and they should!), there will be a period when some suggestions are more acceptable when made by someone other than a teenager's own parents. (Our teenagers got permanents when a girl friend told them they needed something done to their hair.) At times, teenagers are so set on asserting their independence that they will automatically reject any idea that comes from their mother or father. Often they will confide in a teacher, a coach, an older sister, a friend or even a friend's parent. And, from such friends they will frequently take advice that they would reject if it came from their own parents.

I had thought my teenagers were going to bypass this "be suspicious of parents" stage completely. But before I knew it, the two teenagers were organized against the rest of the household. It was as if they had formed a union and gone in for collective bargaining. I had to take stock of the changed situation.

My own parents had tended to be conservative in religion, politics and standards. In my middle teens I tended to be liberal, and many were the arguments we had. I had been prepared to deal with my teenagers as I had earlier wanted to be dealt with. Now I realized I would have to do a different kind of preparation in order to deal with them as they, in their age, needed and wanted to be dealt with.

This experience occurred the year after I started teaching in public school again. I was assigned to the same high school which our second daughter attended. She was glad to get a ride to and from school, but after the ride she would hardly acknowledge me on campus. Some of my students might shout a loud "Hello, Mrs. Garrison" as I walked across the campus, but my own daughter would generally turn her head the other way so she would not have to see me. Students I didn't even know would offer to help me when I was carrying a huge load of books or magazines, but my daughter would rush away from the car as soon as we got to school. I might have been deeply hurt. However, I tried to put myself in my daughter's place. Then I realized how impossible it was for her to acknowledge a teacher as a mother. From this experience I learned how important it was to my daughter to be seen in school as a self-responsible person, and how important it was for me not to "mother" her away from home.

The experience of recommending the home permanent helped me to see that as children reach teen age they resent unasked-for advice. A wise parent keeps silent, knowing that if previous training has been good, her child will accept the very suggestion she wants to make from someone else, or he will reach the same decision under his own steam. Another experience taught me that, though I had to make a point now and then, my teenagers would be apt to accept it more quickly if I didn't press it.

I tried to tell one daughter that other parents of teenagers would not let their youth come to a party she was planning unless they knew her parents. "Oh, nobody's as strict as you," was the retort. Several friends turned down her party invitation because their parents would not let them come. After that catastrophe my daughter began leaving me the phone numbers of her friends' parents. By trial and error she learned that it was far easier to get all the friends she wanted to a party if their mothers had first visited with me over the phone.

Being parents of teenagers is a challenge and a delight. It is fun to watch your own teenagers grow. I found that the fun increases when you let yourself start learning and growing with them.

14

What Teenagers Think of Adults

AT A DAY-LONG MEETING for Camp Fire leaders one fall, a minister, popular with teenagers, was asked to speak to the mothers on "Training Spiritual and Moral Values in Children." To the surprise of everyone, he did not begin with a recital of statistics on juvenile delinquency; instead he began with an indictment of adults. He cited examples of income-tax evasions, little "white lies," quiz-program scandals, business dishonesty, divorce statistics, etc. "No wonder our young people are confused," he said, "when so many adults are giving them patterns they can't live by. If we want our children to keep out of difficulty, we must give them a purpose so strong that it dominates their life." It is herein we have failed, he insisted. We have given our children material luxuries and advantages, but so often we have failed to give meaning to their lives.

At that time, young people had not yet begun to rebel on our campuses; later young people were speaking loudly and clearly about their rebellion.

Under no circumstances dò I justify violence, yet our schools and our adults, as well as our young people, need to make some changes.

My experience has been that many teenagers would echo this minister's viewpoint. The first year I started teaching again in high school some of the boys who were the biggest problems to me had parental problems. One boy in an English essentials class started out well in the fall, and I had hopes of his doing well enough to enter the college preparatory class soon, but by June he was hovering between a D- and an F, when he was capable of doing B work.

That school year his parents were getting a divorce. Early in the year he was involved in an accident (not his fault) in which an elderly person was killed. His mother was in Europe and his father did not seem to be available to help him through this difficult emotional time. For the rest of the year his work steadily deteriorated, and he delighted in making cynical remarks about people's motives and family life.

Another boy, with a brilliant IQ, had never lived up to his potential and already was a year behind his classmates. His life had been torn up emotionally by his mother's many marriages. An accident around Christmastime in which he was injured and his brother was killed seemed to jar him loose from his drifting, and by June he was making an effort to comply with regulations and to learn something.

Perhaps the biggest criticism teenagers make of

adults is that they don't practice what they preach. Twice in the Epistle to the First Corinthians the apostle Paul directly encouraged believers to imitate him. Once he said, "Be imitators of me, as I am of Christ" (I Corinthians 11: 1). Few teaching devices are as effective as leaving a good example for someone else to follow. To Timothy he gave a clear instruction to do the same thing: "Let no one despise your youth, but set the believers an example in speech and conduct, in love, in faith, in purity." Being a worthy example is the responsibility of every parent.

Of course, practicing what one preaches is not nearly as easy as it seems from the Olympian heights of youth. For example, in our own family, both my husband and I are apt to be more critical of the children who have our own faults because we know the danger of our faults.

Young people are inclined to be most critical of adults who do not set a standard worth following, and this fact is true even of young people whose lives are far from exemplary. Marijuana users may insist that their parents are worse with their use of cigarettes and liquor. Often the students who are in the most difficulty at school will be the most critical of teachers, parents and other adults. Part of this criticism, to be sure, is the old technique of shifting the blame. However, many young people are quite just in their remarks.

I remember Kathleen, when she was in the seventh grade, naively remarking of a friend's mother who was divorced, "I know why she was divorced by her husband. She tells lies. When they don't get up in time for Molly to get to school, her mother just writes a note that Molly is sick. Her mother is always making excuses that aren't true."

On the other side of the coin, even though young people are critical of adults and their standards, there are certain occupations or people whom they consider glamorous or "with it," and these people have tremendous influence over their thinking for both good and bad. Often these adults give good, thoughtful advice, but frequently people in glamorous professions or in the arts may be very shallow in their thinking and unexemplary in their conduct.

My seventh-grade Camp Fire Girls were thrilled to start off the year with a charm course, and used most of their club treasury and their allowances to pay for it. The leader of the course was a model, a charming person, who was the picture of grace in every movement.

Although few of the girls realized it, they had been receiving much of her advice for years from their mothers: the value of good posture, correct eating habits, care of clothes, thoughtfulness. They ignored the advice when it came from their parents, but it became gospel truth when it was taught in connection with modeling by a person who was a model.

Young people tend to question many of the old values, sometimes through inexperience, and sometimes through a genuine desire to cut out the useless foliage. When Marilynne was in junior college, my husband asked her if she had taken time to fill out an application for the scholarship society, Alpha Gamma Sigma. "I'm not sure I want to," she replied. "What does the group do except sit around and congratulate each other on being intelligent?"

My husband was understandably miffed at Marilynne's cursory judgment of the scholarship group without her having any real knowledge of it. However, there was a lot to be said for her point of view. She was active in the college-age church group, taught in the junior high department of the Sunday school, had a sixth-grade Camp Fire group, wanted her share of good times and parties and there were a number of clubs that interested her. Did she have time for something purely honorary if it served no other purpose?

We adults devote too much time to show—in publicity of our good works. No young person is interested in doing things just because his parents did. A church cannot challenge him if it doesn't have something to offer other than "punch and cookies." It must get down to real issues and affect people's lives.

With their ruthless questioning of old traditions, youth have often made real improvement in customs. Frequently now sororities and fraternities, instead of making an initiation something of "horse play," have filled community needs in helping to beautify vacant lots or recreation areas, by painting houses of elderly retired people on a small annuity, or by adopting a foreign child through Save the Children or Foster Parents Plan.

Our children's attitudes toward adults can be a real challenge to us as parents. True, they often rebel against authority and question tradition needlessly. Sometimes the people in glamorous jobs that they admire are not worthy of admiration. However, real progress has been made in human relations through their questioning. They want adults whom they can admire, and much of their disillusionment comes because adults frequently do things that are shoddy or cruel. As adults, we need to constantly ask ourselves if our behavior and ideals are what we would like to have our youth emulate.

15

Up and Down

THERE WAS A MOMENT OF SILENCE after the final scene of the dramatic play, "I Have Spoken to My Children," presented by the high school department of the church. Parents and friends had gathered to see the dress rehearsal before a busload of young people took the play on tour to other churches in their area during Easter vacation.

The silence was broken by Jim's mother remarking, "I didn't know Jim had it in him to do such a serious part. He's always such a clown. That play has a real message." I nodded and smiled. Sharon had played a serious part as the mother in the play, and had played it with dignity. Yet we exchanged knowing glances and smiles as we remembered how Sharon had looked the day before, rehearsing, dressed in Bermuda shorts, her hair bulky in big rollers. We remembered Jim as he looked last summer when he had come to a church recreation night, barefoot and bareheaded, forever acting the clown.

One of the confusing facts about a teenager is

that he can be an adult one minute and a child the next. This fact often amazes parents, as it amazed us two mothers, both schoolteachers and both with large families. No matter how much you study academically about teenagers, their amazing changes in real life astonish you.

Of course, it would be foolish to think that we adults never have our ups and downs. We can do a fair job of vacillating between responsible and immature behavior, too.

Think how much Peter must have frustrated Jesus by his moods and impulsiveness. On one occasion Peter expressed genuine concern about how long he should continue forgiving someone for an offense; another time he quickly took to his sword and cut off Malchus' ear. And we all know the familiar story of his boast that he would never forsake Jesus, only to deny even knowing Him just a few hours later.

Most of us are like this at times, but the teen years are especially bewildering to parents because we see a few instances of mature behavior and assume that will be the pattern for the days ahead. Then we feel let down by an immature decision. We must learn that the variation is normal; it is our expectation that was unrealistic.

In a way, the teen years are similar to the two-year-old stage. A two-year-old is changing from babyhood to childhood. A teenager is changing from childhood to adulthood. At both ages, individuals feel the need to assert themselves and proclaim independence. The two-year-old may refuse to take help in dressing or feeding himself and will take forever to perform a simple job, but how else can he learn?

The teenager may refuse to take adult suggestions. He may insist on making his own decisions and, in doing so, be woefully inefficient or careless. Yet, how else can he learn to be on his own? The two-year-old has learned the fun of saying "no." The teenager loves to argue. The two-year-old has learned to say "mine" and finds it difficult to share. At times the teenager seems unbelievably selfish and inconsiderate of the rights of others in the family.

The two-year-old stage is easier to take because it is of shorter duration and because so recently the offspring was a baby. A baby's behavior is excusable on the basis of innocence, but the assertiveness of a teenager cannot be that easily accepted. Parents, nevertheless, must watch their children go through this stage too, and help them grow as they do.

Basically, the technique of handling a teenager is not unlike that of handling a two-year-old. Just as we give the two-year-old a chance to cut out the cookies, dress himself and feed himself, we must give the teenager an opportunity to make many of his own decisions, pick out his own clothes, choose his friends and entertainment.

You need faith in God and a great deal of self-control to give your teenager this freedom and independence. Those past years of Christian training will have made their mark on the teen's life, but you must leave it with God in that moment when your teenager is going to make some decision on his or her own. You hope and pray that it will be made on the basis of Christian principles, but you really can't force it or you will have taken the growth opportunity away from your teen.

Just as we have to expect sticky woodwork when the two-year-olds cut out cookies, so we need to expect some mishaps when the teenager is learning independence. Just as the two-year-old seems at times to slip back into babyhood with feeding habits and dressing, so a teenager seems very immature at times with his lack of planning, sloppy dressing or moods and temper. We need to make opportunities for him to learn independence, just as we did for the two-year-old. If the youngster follows usual patterns, he will behave more and more responsibly while his periods of childish behavior decrease.

What are some of the ways of learning independence? One way is in managing a clothes allowance. Each of the seven in our family, from ten-year-old Bob to Dad himself, had the same microscopic allowance for clothes and cleaning—$5 a month. (In the early years it was only $15 a month for the whole family.) To stay within that strict allowance has always meant careful budgeting—watching sales, mending, sewing and spot-cleaning. The three teenagers were free at any time to take their clothing allowance to shop for items they needed.

If anyone, including the parents, wanted to

indulge in a pet extravagance, he had to pay for it out of extra earnings from baby-sitting, gardening, sale of an article, or, for my husband, an extra encyclopedia sale. Our teenagers learned habits of responsibility and buying that they carried over into adult life.

Teenagers also like responsibility on jobs, without constant adult interference and advice. When David was 14 he had complete charge of the yard. He cleaned it thoroughly, cut the lawn, planted the flowers and responsibly told his father when he needed him to take rubbish down to the dump. In the days in which we first moved to this house, I cut the lawn and Irving trimmed it. Then, when I started back to work, we paid Dave a little extra to take over complete responsibility. It looked much better than it ever did under our supervision. A few years later, with the prospect of both boys away at college, Irving was wondering how he'd ever keep the yard as nicely as they had.

Teenagers also want independence in planning their vocations and choosing their schools. One mother had always hoped some of her children would choose the college she had attended. When she spoke too strongly in favor of it, her two oldest sons were not interested. Then she remembered how unasked-for advice so easily sounds like "let me make up your mind." She wisely left it up to the youngsters to investigate college and write for information.

Sometimes it seems as if teenagers selfishly insist that life must revolve around them. In certain situations, adults and young children can feel rather resentful about the teenager's insistence that he won't go on this picnic or visit that aunt, or that he must be brought back early from the family's vacation because . . . well, because he "has plans."

However, just when others are about convinced that the teenagers are entirely selfish and self-centered, they may surprise everyone with displays of generosity and world concern. In a church high school department the young people became so concerned after hearing a woman speak on needs in Africa that they organized a car wash to raise money for the cause that speaker was representing. Recently two teenagers found they were earning more than was usual and that their church pledges did not take a tenth of their income. They began putting a tenth of their extra money in a joint piggy bank, and are now trying to decide how best they can help in relieving world misery: by giving to various missionaries, world relief, or some other project.

One of the high school service clubs is helping in a nursery school, painting a playhouse and assisting in medical drives. At a recent city election, high school people checked off names at the polls and contacted people who had not voted.

These evidences of concern and generosity are the more worthy because they are spontaneous and voluntary. They truly represent the free, un-manipulated responses of teenagers to needs other than their own.

Since teenagers are constantly changing back and

forth from childhood to adulthood, their changes are confusing to adults who are trying to label them as mature or immature. One high school teacher was talking with some other teachers at a recent senior prom. "Can you believe that these well-behaved, beautifully dressed couples are the same sloppy, childish kids we see every day in class?" she asked. If a teenager is given an opportunity to develop responsibility, more and more his actions will be those of a mature person. The older teen, if he is given the chance, will behave in a mature way most of the time.

The teen age, with its change from childhood to adulthood, is not an easy age, but it is never boring. It is fascinating to watch character develop, and appalling when, at times, it seems to shrink and die. Strong-willed, impatient parents, who like things to happen definitely and fast, will not find this an easy stage to see their youngsters through. They may be helped by remembering the infinite patience of God who labors on through the eons, perfecting His creations. As we remember God's patience for centuries, our impatience over the few teen years seems trivial.

Each time a teenager accepts and masters a new responsibility, he takes a step forward into maturity and, hopefully, toward God.

16

Love Your Teenager

I DON'T SEE WHY a teenager has to turn everything into an argument," said Helen plaintively to the adult church school class. The members were discussing the particular problems of parents with teenagers. "I come home from work tired, eager for a little peace and quiet, and Bill has to argue over everything I tell him."

There was general laughter. "Bill is just starting his teenage years," said one father. "Brace yourself. You have at least five more years to go."

"What are you complaining about?" asked a mother of three teenagers. "You have just one child."

Because the minister to youth, employed temporarily for the summer, was so popular with the young people, he had been asked to speak to the monthly adult forum group on the topic, "Understanding Your Teenagers." Part of his popularity could be explained by his good looks, the parents of the girls thought privately. However, he had had experience working in settlement houses and had just graduated from a divinity school. In the fall he was going to continue his graduate studies in clinical psychology and psychotherapy.

When the young minister had thrown the meeting open to questions, Helen had been the first to speak. Laughter greeted her words, but it was rueful laughter, caused by shared experiences. There wasn't a parent at the meeting who had not at some time or another complained that his teenager made an argument out of everything.

Often, in his desire to form his own opinions and make his own personality, a teenager resists authority—whether it is the authority of the parents, the school or the church. Because he has the tremendous drive to "establish his own identity," he tends to be argumentative in expressing his opinions.

Perhaps one of the values of a discussion group is the realization that comes to each parent that other parents are facing identical problems. Some laughed with Helen and thought of their own teenagers. Everything has to be a debate, even the simplest statements:

"You're getting a cold."

"No, I'm not, I just have the sniffles."

"Your library books are overdue."

"No, they aren't. I didn't get a ride to school yesterday when I planned to return them, and they were too heavy to carry."

"Your slip is showing."

"No, it isn't. The lace on the hem is just torn."

It is difficult to live with, but a parent has more

cause for worry if there is never any conflict. Differences of opinion are all a part of growing up and gaining independence.

This is no plea for teenage license. When the question is something that could permanently affect a teenager's health, morals or preparation for life work, then a parent needs to assert his authority. Within reason, however, it is good for a teenager to make his own decisions and then accept the consequences of those decisions when he makes a mistake. If a teenager buys his own clothes (and few teenagers will tolerate their parents' choices), he should just wear his mistakes and should not be rescued from poor decisions by additional funds.

Out of a concern to help their child escape punishment, some parents are constantly rescuing their teenager from trouble. This help is unfair to the teenager, for he will learn nothing about making his own decisions unless he accepts the consequences. God, as a Heavenly Father, lets us learn from our mistakes. It is an orderly universe, and He does not break the law of the universe to rescue us. As parents, we need to beware of rescuing except when there will be permanent bad effects from a decision, or when the happiness and welfare of other persons are affected.

The desire to plan one's own schedule and the argumentative quality that Helen was talking about are characteristics of most teenagers. Parents need empathy, the ability to put themselves in another's place. In dealing with teenagers, they need to remember themselves as they were growing up, recalling the desire to do their own thinking and to make their own decisions. They need to remember that as teenagers they found their own parents "difficult." If a parent gives his child a sound background of Christian values from babyhood on, if he shows him love and understanding during this trying time, his teenager may often surprise him with his mature understanding of a problem or his ability to carry through a difficult situation. When it appears a youngster is certainly going to muff a responsibility, parents should not habitually jump in to save him from his own folly. By really learning through experience now the consequences of such follies as "putting it off," the teenager may mend his ways of going at things and be saved from carrying indolent habits on into adulthood.

With the teen age, as with all ages, Christian love and empathy are the magic that dissolves barriers and opens doors to satisfying interpersonal relationships. Of all the answers "experts" can suggest to parents who have problems with their teenagers, this is the first: "Love them, and be channels through which God loves them."

17

Understanding Parents of Teenagers (and Yourself Too!)

REAMS HAVE BEEN WRITTEN about understanding your teenager. Reams have been written about juvenile delinquency and the parents' responsibility. But what about understanding the parents of teenagers? What has been said to give the parents of perfectly normal, decent teenagers the courage to live through the years when they are misunderstood and misquoted and nagged? For parents are people too!

A number of years ago I remember a minister saying, "No matter how experienced you are in working with young people, this thing hits you. Our oldest daughter was always adjustable, and when she first became a teenager, she was still thoughtful and considerate. I decided that people who talked about teenage problems lacked understanding. Then our youngest daughter became a teenager, and suddenly nothing I did satisfied either daughter. You have to live through this time to understand other people's problems." His experience was our experience a few years later.

What causes normal, decent children who were delightful youngsters to change into touchy, disagreeable teenagers? What are some of the attitudes a parent may expect? It helps a person to realize that he is not alone, that all parents of teenagers are going through the same problems. Unless the parent of teenagers realizes that everyone is experiencing the same thing, he feels so alone and so stupid. He keeps asking himself, "What did I do to bring this dissension on myself?"

Most normal younger children tend to look up to their parents, and even when they are angry with them, they do not seriously question their authority or ability. But as they get older, they gain enough perception to see that their parents have made mistakes, that sometimes their judgment was not good, and frequently in some fields the teenager's knowledge surpasses his parents'. Particularly is that true in the fields of science and the new math. Teenagers may be better informed on some subjects, but they have not yet gained enough maturity to be tolerant of other people's faults.

Because they have discovered that their former idols have feet of clay, suddenly nothing the parents do is right. Also, since much of the teenagers' knowledge is theoretical, rather than based on experience, they are extremely critical of any deviation from the ideal, due to practical considerations. Suddenly every meal should look like a magazine illustration, regardless of the budget or mother's diet. The house which before was satisfying if it was colorful and a source of fun must suddenly look like a model home. Younger brothers and sisters who were formerly adored are now considered "unmannerly, dirty little brats." If straight hair is in style, mother is old-fashioned if she clings to a style that is more comfortable and practical for her way of life. After the teenagers have had a course in drivers' education, it is evident that father does not always watch the speed laws and mother does not signal vigorously enough or long enough in advance of turning. Teenagers have overdeveloped critical faculties. Nothing you can do pleases them, and they see all your mistakes and comment on them.

Second, people who ordinarily are even-tempered, become quarrelsome. Often in junior high, teenage girls have quarrels with their best friends and may not be on speaking terms for three months. They insist they did not provoke the quarrel, and then inadvertently drop a remark that makes you wonder how they have a friend left. Teenagers tend to argue with younger brothers and sisters, and often they refuse to associate with anyone who is not their own age.

Third, during the teenage years, advice from any other adult is preferable to advice from one's parents. Anybody else's brothers and sisters are preferable to one's own. "Familiarity breeds contempt," and no man can be a hero to his teenage son or daughter.

Part of this disenchantment with one's parents is natural and necessary. If children are to grow into

111

mature adults who stand on their own feet and make their own decisions, they must to a certain extent break with their parents. Until the break is firmly established, they must of necessity reject more firmly ideas and suggestions from their parents than from other adults. Because they are struggling to maintain their own identity, they may reject ideas you have worked for. If you're liberal, they may become the most reactionary conservatives or vice versa. Your church is no longer satisfying. They want to join another church or they don't understand why people go to church at all. Other friends who don't attend church have had their children become ardent churchgoers and talk of training for the ministry.

But what help is there for the bewildered parent? How can he get through these difficult years without utterly losing his self-confidence? Realistically, he must find the answer himself or learn it from other parents. Many books are written on "understanding your teenager," but how many acknowledge that parents are people, too?

First, try to remember your own teenage years. Were you difficult to live with? I know I caused my parents concern. Because I tended to be more liberal in my outlook than anyone else in the family, I was very critical of people who thought differently. It took being on my own to make me realize that my parents were right in many areas, and even though we still disagreed in some respects, I became mature enough to give them their right to their own opinions. After I recovered from my own teenage rebellion, there has been no one whose company I have enjoyed more than that of my own parents.

Second, only the old cliches seem to work in times of real stress, and since "misery loves company," the parents of teenagers need to compare notes with other parents. Then they'll discover that they are not the only ones who feel inadequate. A parent may even find that other parents have more difficult problems than he does. Somehow, the knowledge that the stress is not due entirely to his own bungling, helps sustain him over difficult moments.

Third, parents need to develop their own interests and hobbies. When children are little, parents expend so much energy in getting all the work done that they often neglect hobbies that have meaning for them. Now is the time to get out the old tennis racket, the typewriter and manuscript envelopes, the painting pallette, or to start practicing the piano. Developing a skill can help banish feelings of inferiority.

It may be a time for mothers to get a part-time job. Many of my friends have been going back to school, brushing up on shorthand, renewing their teaching credentials. Even if your children don't want your help now, other agencies do.

Parents need to develop their own social life. If the children no longer want family outings or family parties, now is the time to do things with other couples, to join a community group, to polish up on games, to attend some of the concerts that you couldn't afford when the whole family wanted to go with you.

Finally, when things are most difficult, remind yourself: "This too shall pass."

18

Plan for When the Birds Start Flying

WHEN OUR CHILDREN WERE EIGHT, six, four, two, and six months old, nothing annoyed me more than to find an article, written by some *man,* stating that women didn't have enough to do and needed some worthwhile activity to fill their leisure time. *What* leisure time? True, those who could afford it (I didn't even have an automatic washer at that time) did have more conveniences than their parents, but their mothers were not expected to do so much in the community and some of them either sent the laundry out or at least had a cleaning woman.

Nine years later, when our children were 17, 15, 13, 11, and 9, I was still not overwhelmed by the leisure on my hands. I could see it coming, however. All of our children were good help, and I was less occupied with the physical necessities of life. Then the question that faced me was: How can I use the remainder of my life to the best advantage and so that I can be of the most service? It is a question that is facing many women as they pass from the younger to the older generation.

Many women never faced that problem because they took jobs to augment the family income as soon as their children could walk. Except for the emergencies of war, illness, or a husband's education, however, I have always felt it was more important to have a vital part in our children's training than to have a larger income. Other women waited until their children were in school before taking full-time jobs. Is this the answer? How much help should a working mother have if she is to have time for her family?

A full-time job was not the answer for me, at least not at first. I think teenagers need relaxed, happy mothers, ready for parties and friends dropping in, even more than the preschoolers do. Our younger children needed Camp Fire and Indian Guides even more than they needed a larger income. Perhaps having a Camp Fire group and teaching Sunday school at that time made as much contribution to the community as a job. Seventeen years ago in May, when I was in the hospital for an emergency operation, I decided it was time I did a little thinking about how I wanted to live the remainder of my life. It was near the end of school, and it had been the first school year that all five children had been in school. Somehow I had allowed my schedule to become overloaded. People were always saying, "Now that all your children are in school, you must do this," and I hadn't yet learned how to say "no" without my children for an excuse.

Once I was over the pain and through the 11

days with a tube down my throat, my main reaction was one of relief. Surely now people could not expect me to do quite so many things. Maybe I would have a chance just to enjoy living for a change. But I was mistaken. While I was still going to the doctor for weekly checkups, work committees were meeting in my home so that I "wouldn't have to go out."

Before the summer was over I had accepted a job teaching Christian weekday education two days a week, partly because I was vitally concerned and partly to get out of some of my obligations for PTA and other community affairs. A part-time job interrupts a family less than endless committee meetings. Because I found the job extremely challenging, it was the answer for me for three years. Then I decided I needed to continue the thinking I had started three years before and decide if I were on the path I wanted to take. Since I enjoy more mature minds, should I renew my high school credentials and go back to teaching?

I looked around me at friends my age or ten years older and thought of the direction they had taken. Was it the direction I wanted to take? Had their lives been enriched without hurting their families? Was I doing what I was intended to do, or was I just drifting? Did I need to wait until all my children were nearly through school to do what I really wanted to do? Was there any training or preparation I could be doing at the time?

These are questions that all mothers need to ask as their children get more independent. They are

117

not easy questions for a woman whose family is more important than professional status.

Even in 1960 I could look around me and see several friends who had solved their futures to their own satisfaction. One friend had been a social worker before she was married. With her children all in school, she wanted some outside stimulus besides church and PTA, and yet social work demanded too long hours to leave her the time she wanted for her family. She began to observe her children's classes and make lesson plans as if she were teaching them. After she had gotten some credits in education, she told the school personnel office that she was available for substitute work two or three times a week. Her ability in managing a class soon became so evident that her biggest problem was turning down work because she did not want to teach more than half time.

Another friend had never really enjoyed housework, but had done her job faithfully while the children were small. Her interest in newspaper work led her to writing publicity for a hospital; and by the time her children were in junior high through college, she had a full-time job managing a hospital. She hired a maid to come in each afternoon to do the housework, start dinner and be there when the children came home from school. Because housework was not enjoyable to her, a full-time job with part-time help became her answer.

One friend with six children saw the need for extra income as her oldest girl grew near college age. She had done an excellent job with her own children and was so inspired in Sunday school teaching that everyone said she was a born teacher. She finished the training she needed, and then started in as a preschool teacher. Eventually as her children did not need her so much she became a very successful elementary schoolteacher.

Another friend, who was a teacher before she was married, found herself more interested in politics through her lawyer husband's concerns. Even with two preschoolers, she managed to do a great deal of political entertainment. When her children became older, she was appointed by the governor to several school committees.

A neighbor, whose husband had formerly been a newspaper columnist, always wanted to write. When all of her children were in school, she began doing book reviews for the newspaper for which her husband had worked. Eventually her reviews were important enough that they were given a by-line.

A former neighbor, who loves children and who had the relaxed but firm temperament necessary, started doing child care and is licensed to look after six children. Lucky are the children who are in her care, for they have a real home atmosphere. There are even birthday and Christmas parties.

Another friend, whose three children are all married, became interested in education when she was a PTA president. As her children grew up, she obtained her teaching credentials and now teaches in the school where she was once PTA president.

Each woman must seek the answer for herself. The answer will vary with families, husband's attitude, her own temperament and training, financial needs and values. But as children of a family mature, there are several paths a mother might take.

Many will want to take the path of community responsibility. Our communities could not function without the unselfish service of women through Community Chest, Red Cross, missionary societies, cultural organizations, PTA and youth groups. I had found Camp Fire and teaching a Sunday school class challenging, but the path I eventually took led to a regular job.

A job presents questions for any woman. During the years when a mother's first responsibilities are to a family, how can she keep up with her training? There are many services she can perform that will use her ability. A bookkeeper or secretary would be welcomed as a treasurer of any organization. Camp Fire, Sunday school teaching and writing helped me in the techniques of teaching high school English.

Regardless of which path she intends to take, a woman needs to take careful thought if she is to make those years when "the birds begin to fly" rich and useful ones.

19

Traditions Can Be Fun

You don't have to have come over on the Mayflower to build up traditions in your family. Nor do you have to be gray with age to want something done in the accustomed way. A kindergartner may declare, "That's not the way our family does it." A new bride and groom may carry over ideas from their respective homes, or may decide on certain traditions they want to establish in their home. Traditions, like clothes and homes, should reflect personality and vary from family to family. What sort of traditions do you want to start in your family? What traditions do you want in your neighborhood? You might get some ideas from what other people do.

Our neighbor celebrates Thanksgiving the Sunday before, and has over not only family and in-laws but close friends. We were fortunate to be included in the group of 24 she had this year; the number grows larger each year as the great-grandchildren are starting to appear. Family pictures of previous years are part of the fun.

Another family makes Christmas a craft time. In November they start by using old Christmas cards for decorations or for that year's gift tags or decorations. There are family craft nights of making candles, baking cookies, making candy and other gifts.

Another family enjoys armchair traveling. Every three months they choose another country to study. A map is pinned to the family bulletin board, and they begin to collect travel folders, pictures and books. The mother experiments with fixing a few dishes of the country, and a foreign student visiting from that country is invited to the home for dinner.

Another family had made a summer camping trip part of its tradition. Much of the year is spent in discussing places to visit and routes to take. Pop polishes up his pancake technique and Junior learns to concoct a "mean hobo stew."

We have carried over from my home a tradition of making each birthday an exciting affair, and our two married daughters have followed the same tradition. In my childhood home the person celebrating his birthday was excused from any of his regular chores—doing dishes, dusting, etc.—and he could always (within reason) choose his birthday dinner. Of course, there were birthday gifts from everyone in the family.

Another family tradition we have kept is the love of games. I can remember my parents playing games with me, and our children are equally fond of games. One of the reasons they love vacation is that there is more time to play together as a family. In good weather the Ping-Pong table is always up in the patio. The bounce of the ball gives me a slight nostalgic feeling, for our children are using the table that my father made for us as children. Although my father has been dead for 16 years now, I can still remember his relentless return of the ball so that he wore opponents out by his consistent playing.

In my husband's family the tradition of music is strong, and he has taught each of our children to play some instrument. In addition, family attendance at a musical event is always celebrated with refreshments. My husband is insistent on hearing the children's performances, and even drove 65 miles to our daughter's college to hear her play the oboe in the orchestra's program.

Because even the fondest of relatives may hesitate some about asking a family of seven over for dinner, many of our family traditions center on our entertaining on the holidays.

Traditions can even make traveling with five children more palatable. Camp songs, lustily sung, make a trip go more quickly. Guests in the car were quickly initiated into the game of pig or donkey or geography. While the rest of the country condemns billboards, we used them; we divided into teams and collected the alphabet (in order) from first letters of words in billboards. Or we each chose our favorite brand of filling station to see who could collect the most in a trip.

Does your family have any traditions? If it

doesn't, why not start building some now, for a school or a business or a home commands more loyalty as it begins to establish meaningful traditions.

20

Make Thanksgiving a Tradition

IS THANKSGIVING JUST A TIME of turkey and trimmings to your family, or does it mean something more than food? Worthwhile family traditions help to make any holiday memorable. Traditions don't have to be original—ours are not—but they do need to fit your family. We have two traditions that have come to mean *Thanks*giving to us.

Somewhere I read that Thanksgiving ought to be a time of writing letters of appreciation to people who have made a genuine contribution to your family. The first year I wrote our letters I felt a little foolish, but the response was most gratifying. I wrote to the doctor who had delivered two of our babies, thanking him for the pleasantness of periodic office checkups and for the ease and reasonableness with which he had handled difficult births. Almost immediately we received an appreciative letter back from him, saying that in all the time he had been practicing medicine this was the first time that anyone had written to thank him.

We also wrote to my parents, thanking them for their hospitality to me and the children during the war when we had housing difficulties, and for their understanding of my irritable moods when I was missing my husband. This letter seemed to leave the difficult war years as pleasant memories for both families.

Each year, in picking two friends to whom letters should go, we recalled the many pleasant things people had done for our family, and realized how much we owe to other people. There was the friend who had no children of her own, and often volunteered to look after our children when we went for outings. Another friend had contributed to our spiritual growth by sharing books that had been meaningful in her religious life. My sister, who always volunteered to look after our children when we were adding another baby to our household, came in for thanks. A minister who had stimulated our thinking and helped us find a closer walk with God deserved appreciation. A dentist who kept charges down to prewar prices earned our heartfelt gratitude.

Each family has its own group of friends and acquaintances who have made contributions to its life. Let's make Thanksgiving a time to thank them. Appreciation means so much to people. And the habit of appreciating can do so much for us.

The Thanksgiving dinner is usually held at our house. Remembering how much as children we enjoyed entertainment mixed in with food, we have two ceremonies with dinner. Between the tomato juice cocktail and the carving of the turkey we have one-minute humorous talks—based on typed topics the guests find under their water glasses. Between the main course and dessert, we do more talking to regain our appetites. Each person thanks God for the nice things that have happened during the year.

I remember the one year that we thought none of us could be thankful and we wondered if we could even have a Thanksgiving dinner. My father had died unexpectedly of a heart attack just the week before. Mother said to go ahead with the dinner—that children count on holidays. When the day came, she discovered that it was easier to be with her family than alone. At first we planned to omit both sets of talks. Then we remembered the first Thanksgiving. The Pilgrims had met many hardships. Many of their dear ones had died. Yet they thanked God for the blessings they did have, and looked forward with faith and courage in God and the future. Could we do less?

As each person thanked God for the blessings of the year, we discovered it had really been, up to the last week, a most satisfying year for all of us. Mother could rejoice that Dad had not suffered, had in fact been laughing at the moment his heart stopped beating. That very evening he had been anticipating the family Thanksgiving celebration and recounting his blessing to prove that it had been one of the happiest years of his life.

21

Christmas in Your Heart

WHEN THE CHILDREN WERE LITTLE, each year I was
beguiled by articles and editorials urging me not to
let Christmas be a busy, rushed season, but a time
of peace and quiet beauty. Every year I would
resolve that it would be different next Christmas
and that I would not still be addressing Christmas
cards a few days before the event and wrapping
presents and making doll clothes up to midnight
on Christmas Eve. I would get such a frustrated
feeling, trying not to be hurried, and I would wonder if I should not have had fewer children or
chosen a husband who didn't leave everything until the last moment if I were to have a quiet,
leisurely holiday season.

One Christmas I suddenly rebelled. I decided
that those who advocated the quiet, restful life had
no small children. Anything worth achieving takes
hard work, and the great accomplishments of the
world are not made by those who are searching for
the balanced life or peace of mind or leisure. Any
wife and mother of young children finds her daily

schedule of meals, washing, ironing, cleaning, mending, sewing, teaching and supervising a busy one. Add to her household jobs a regular contribution to the community. If anything unexpected, such as illness, comes along, her time becomes even more fully scheduled. How can Christmas—with church and school activities, gift selections and entertaining—be anything but busy? Any mother who thinks life for her can be leisurely and quiet is asking for frustration and irritation. She needs to recognize that—for her—life will of necessity be busy, and she needs to feel joy in the contribution she can make to the happiness of the community and her family.

How did the idea originate that Christmas was a time of quiet and peace? The original Christmas was anything but restful, and not all of the arrangements were the best. What woman would want to travel miles to a crowded city at the time her baby was due? How well did Mary and Joseph plan their trip that they were unable to get a room at the inn? Other people had managed to get there in time for proper lodging. Was it a restful trip for the shepherds? They had to leave their sheep, and add a trip to their regular duties. The Wise Men, too, made a tremendously long journey and spent years studying the stars so that they might know when to follow the star to the Christ Child. Once Jesus was born, was Mary able to have the rest and tranquillity a new mother deserves? No, for fear of Herod, they could not return home, but had to journey to Egypt.

Why then do we get an impression of peace when the original Christmas was so full of changed plans, rush, the bustle and commotion of an over-crowded town? It was because peace was in the hearts of the people concerned. They had found fulfillment in service and in something bigger than themselves. Peace is an attitude of mind, not a matter of external circumstances. Constantly in Jesus' ministry crowds pressed about Him when He tried to be alone; His teachings were misunderstood; and His enemies tried to trap Him. Yet, throughout all the complexities of His life, His spirit was tranquil; He was poised, and His outlook on people was loving.

Is not this the truth for Christmastime—a loving tranquil spirit in the midst of a busy life—rather than a time of leisure and reflection?

How does one get this tranquil spirit in the midst of confusion and noise and busyness? If you have children, there will be confusion, noise and bustle as well as a deep inner joy. Each person must answer that for himself, for inspiration comes in different ways to different people. This one thing I know, however, in busy times no one can afford to neglect a daily "Quiet Time" or prayer or devotional reading.

I would like to mention some of the Christmas traditions we have found meaningful, for I think it is helpful for parents to compare notes.

Our children particularly enjoyed starting the day by reading the devotions in a Christian family magazine which gave the background of so many

131

Christmas traditions. Also, at our evening meal, we made a ceremony of lighting candles for dessert, dropping pennies in a world bank for Meals for Millions or Church World Service, and singing Christmas carols. Even two-year-old Robert had his turn of choosing a song which was invariably "Jesus Loves Me."

One joy of Christmastime is hearing from friends who have been silent throughout the year. The newsy cards and photographs of the family are our favorites. Because we are always disappointed if there is no news with the card, we send mimeographed letters to all our friends whom we don't see often.

We have always felt present-giving should be a personal affair; so as soon as the children were old enough to receive allowances, they have saved for weeks to buy presents. As we watched the children's pride in their own contributions, we felt it was worth the time it took in supervising the shopping and wrapping.

Part of our family tradition was having a Christmas worship service before the younger children went to bed. It generally consisted of the Christmas story, a few carols, a poem or a litany, and a prayer. It helped to put us in the reverent, quiet mood after all the busy preparations of the day.

Eventually the neighborhood Christmas sing evolved out of this custom. Three families, with church interests and small children, take turns having neighborhood families over on Christmas Eve to sing Christmas carols and have simple refreshments. Our daughter in Texas writes that this is one of the traditions she misses most.

Each family has its own traditions at Christmas, its bit of happy memories. Let some of the memories be of cheerful work, sacrificial giving and of family worship, and the heart will be joyful.

22

Family Year With Meaning

PART OF THE FASCINATION of a new baby is that people sense the drama of a new life, a being filled with as yet unknown possibilities. This same excitement is before us at the start of a new year. Perhaps this year we will obtain the sort of family life we have dreamed about.

Will we? Probably not, unless we do a little planning. Living is somewhat like budgeting; unless we plan for the things we want, the big things are usually crowded out by the small things. Just as there is seldom money left over for savings and benevolence if it is not taken out first, there is seldom time left over for prayer or church or family fun if we do not insist on taking that time first when we plan the day or the week. Any family with a number of children must have long-term goals, but it is fun to have immediate goals too, goals for this very year.

New Year's resolutions have long been made the subject of jokes because they are so often broken. Most people find planning goals for the year more rewarding. We tend to become discouraged and quit when we make one slip in our resolution. If we have goals we can always hope that if we work a little harder we can achieve them.

In addition, specific family problems might be touched on for the next year. How can we make our family devotions more meaningful? What suggestions do the children have for cutting down on quarreling? What can we do to make mealtimes enjoyable, times that all of us anticipate with pleasure?

We often make New Year's Eve a candle-lighting service. In our family, after a general discussion of family goals, we bring out a small box saved from last year. Each person reads his goals for the past year and confesses where he has fallen down and where he has made his biggest accomplishments. Sometimes he asks for suggestions from the rest of the family, but unasked-for advice or opinions are not encouraged.

What are some of the goals a family and the individuals in it might have? Goals for living, like budgets, would vary according to the tastes, interests and abilities of each individual family. However, suggested divisions under which goals could fall might be these: money goals, spiritual goals, family activity goals, mental goals, physical goals, and personal goals.

Foremost in a family's money goals should be tithing or proportionate giving, and it can be accomplished only by planning and setting aside a set amount of each paycheck for benevolent purposes.

Anyone who has seen the needs of people in other countries cannot with a free conscience enjoy the plenty of the United States without setting aside a generous portion for the church and for others. If a family can possibly manage it, one interest outside of church contributions adds so much to life.

Money goals for the family may vary from year to year. One year it might mean enlarging the playroom. Another year the family might want to save for a trip together. It might be a goal that involves as much work as money—painting some rooms, refinishing furniture, making family Christmas cards, canning, sewing, tending a garden, raising rare plants, making a stamp collection. As the children get older, saving for college or vocational training must certainly figure in family money plans.

Spiritual goals might be both family and individual. Thoughtful family devotions, adapted to fit the family and the age of the children, can be an important way of starting the day or tying together the day's activities, depending on the family's schedule. Each individual may have some devotional book in addition to the Bible that he wants to study by himself during the year. One year everyone might try to be more thoughtful; another year refraining from criticism may be a family goal.

Perhaps it is because my own parents were so good at playing with their three children that I believe firmly in planning for family fun. In addition to doing things together as a family—Ping-

Pong, picnics, skating, hiking, games—definite "fun" activities might be planned from year to year.

Do we get so bogged down with scheduled meetings that we don't have time to see the friends we really enjoy? Perhaps at the start of the new year the family might make a list of the friends who just can't be neglected during the year. When both adults and children in two families are friends, it is fun to entertain a whole family. The children always have individual friends whom they want as guests for dinner and overnight. Perhaps when a family outing is planned, one child might bring a guest.

Physical goals might be losing weight or gaining weight. Happy is the family with the same problems. Our family is complicated because two members want to lose weight and two want to gain weight and the rest are just interested in eating. Each person may have some health problem that he needs to tackle. Families can have fun exercising together. Bike-riding expeditions are particularly challenging.

Personal goals can vary from year to year. They might include getting a stamp collection organized, sorting through recipes and getting them in order, learning a language, learning to play an instrument, getting elected to an office, attending a concert series, playing in Little League, attending a creative writing class or learning to paint portraits. Whatever the goal, each person needs individual as well as family goals.

The start of a new year is always exciting! The next year can be the most rewarding yet if we take steps toward attaining the goals we have always vaguely dreamed about but have never defined.

23

The Family Goes to Church

I CAN'T GET MY FAMILY to go to church," complained Jan. "The children always want to sleep late because of a party the night before, or they need to do their homework."

"Besides, the service lasts too long," agreed Beth. "You can't expect a young child to sit for two hours, first through Sunday school and then church." (That same child can sit through a double-feature movie twice, and goes to school from nine to three.)

Jan ran her hand distractedly through her hair. "I've tried, I've really tried," she said. "Besides, we get our worship from the great out-of-doors."

Had she really tried? Those who love us gauge our values from how we act as well as what we say. If there is a good relationship, people try to cooperate on things that are mutually important.

I know, for as a young teacher I found all sorts of excuses for not going to church. Sunday morning was the best time to correct papers. I could get more inspiration in 15 minutes with a devotional book than in an hour and a half going to a small-town church.

I found even less time after I was married. But by then I could see church was really important. In fact, if I was too tired (or later, if the children were) to get up early on Sunday, Irving said we really ought to curb our Saturday activities. I discovered he was right. There is a richness from corporate worship that we can get no other way.

I have come to the conclusion that regular attendance of anything is largely habit, and each time we break that habit we are lowering its effectiveness. We are also lowering the effectiveness of a group, for a class in school or in church needs continuity, and group spirit influences everyone. A large group of young people in church stimulates others to come. Family groups sitting together are an inspiration to other families.

Knowing that church is a major priority in life may influence those who love us. What else can we do to make Sunday school and church seem essential to our family?

First, everything should be done to make the scramble on Sunday morning as pleasant as possible. Clothes for the children and their lesson quarterlies can be laid out the night before. If Irving wanted us to leave on time he did not sit out in the car and honk, but helped in supervising the children's dressing.

Second, friendship with church families helped to make church enjoyable for the children. When our children were young, often families would get together after church for picnics in the park or for potluck dinners. Indeed, much of our social life has centered around the church and the friends we have made there.

Third, if your teenagers turn from your church, try to make some adjustment that is amenable to both generations. I can remember as a teenager being very resentful because my parents went to the church of their denomination in a nearby large town and insisted that I go too. Now as an adult, I know their evaluation of the leadership of the two ministers was correct; but then I was miserable, for high schoolers can be cliquish, and my friends went to the small community church. Consequently, when the youth department of our church hit a slump, I suggested that our oldest son go to a nearby church with a large youth group.

Fourth, be willing to help make the Sunday school meaningful for your children. When the children were younger, it was Irving who worked at the elementary level, both because of his experience with that age at school and because the adult class was not as necessary for his morale as it was for mine, since I was more housebound.

Fifth, we must be concerned about what is taught and emphasized in church school and do our part to keep the balance right. Jesus was concerned about the spirit, about prayer, about knowing the Scriptures, and many times the Bible mentions that He went apart to pray. But He also was concerned with people's physical needs; He healed the sick and He fed the hungry. If a church is strong on Bible-reading and prayer but ignores the welfare of God's world, it is missing God's message. However if the emphasis is all on social action and not enough concerned with character and prayer and the Bible, there is no strong foundation on which to build. Young people need both elements in their lives, and the concerned parent should work in his church to maintain this balance.

Sixth, in the home there needs to be an emphasis on tithing of talents and money for God's causes. Although Jesus came to fulfill the Law, He did not demand less of people, but more. Too often, in an effort not to be legalistic, we have tended to deemphasize the Law. People need some sort of yardstick below which they should not fall. If children see their parents take their tithe out of their paycheck, they gain an understanding of the importance of doing their share. If they see their parents giving time and money to the church, they garner an appreciation of its value.

Seventh, parents need to be concerned that youth's needs are being met in an imaginative way in the church. For years our youth choirs were carbon copies of the adult choir, and no one was enthusiastic. In the last five years we have had a youth choir which can sing the classics and does, but which can also sing some of the new Christian songs that are being written in the new modes.

Eighth, a parent needs to be concerned with more than attendance, just as he would in school. It is not enough to have pleasant, agreeable teachers. Is the child learning? Is he gaining an overall picture of the Bible and the continuity of tradition? Is he gaining insights from God's Word that will help him with his everyday living? Is his concern with God's Word prodding him into some constructive social action?

Making the church meaningful to our children is no easy task, but it is worthwhile. Loyalty to Christ's Church can furnish the ballast that so many people need today to withstand the storms of life.

24

Are You a Parasite Parent?

AT THE TEACHERS' MEETING, Hazel ran her hand
wearily through her hair. "I've called every mother
who is not already involved somewhere to help in
the extended session, and I didn't get one person.
It isn't that I don't enjoy the kindergarten children,
but I need to get to either Sunday church school or
the church service one time a month to get inspiration myself."

Mary spoke up. "Call the busy mothers first.
The ones without responsibilities have been avoid-
ing doing anything for years. They will never
help."

"One woman even had the nerve to tell me that
she didn't come to church to get involved," said
Hazel resentfully. "She came to hear the music and
the minister's sermon. I would like to hear a
church service myself once this year instead of
looking after her children."

I laughed. "This isn't just a problem of the
churches, finding enough Sunday school teachers
and mothers to help with the younger children

during church time. We had a Camp Fire leaders' meeting today, and everyone was making the same complaint. They couldn't get the parents to help."

"I know," one of the other teachers agreed. "You would think teaching Sunday school would keep me busy enough, but I have a Brownie group too. We have a station wagon, and I make it a rule never to have more girls in my troop than I can take in my car, because it is too hard to get parents to help with the transportation."

Mary nodded her head. "Parent participation is the biggest problem in any group. My husband has Scouts and they have some of the same problems. Many parents don't even come out to see their children given awards. We are just being used as free baby-sitters.

"Sometimes I feel like dropping the children whose parents never help in anything, but they are always the children who need something like Brownies or Blue Birds or Scouts and especially Church activities."

Several weeks later, when I was taking my Camp Fire group on a hike, I remembered the conversation at the Sunday school teachers' meeting. Dana's remark brought it to mind. As we were hiking, she pointed to the yellow, fibrous growth that practically covered many of the bushes. "What's that?" she asked.

"The common name for it is witches' hair," I told her. "It is a parasite. It has to start on the ground, but once it has made a start, it can grow anywhere, even in the air."

As I answered Dana, I recalled the teachers' meeting and thought how many parents are like parasites. They give their children birth and may even pay for everything the children ask for, but they depend on other people to give them their instruction, amusement and religious training: teachers, Sunday school departments, recreation centers and character education groups.

They are harming their children by being parasite parents, for children learn habits of doing their share by example. They are also harming themselves and missing out on a lot of fun. How often do we read letters written to Dear Abby or some other newspaper columnist, always with the same story, "I'm lonely and it's hard to get acquainted. People in church or clubs are not friendly." The best way to get to know people is to work with them. These same people who are unwilling to help in church activities don't help in the community either, and then complain about things which are wrong. The only way to get a better community or a better world is to work for it.

"But," you say, "I really haven't time to help." You would be surprised at how you can find the time once you actually get started with a group. I thought I did not have time to continue with my ninth-grade Sunday school class when I started teaching two days a week, but the officers were so good about taking over phoning responsibilities that I discovered I could make the time.

Perhaps you really do not have the time or the aptitude to be a Sunday school teacher or a youth group leader. What can you do to help the person who has taken that responsibility? Every parent should manage to attend at least one of the parents' meetings for the Sunday school class and any award meetings involving her child. I have had Blue Birds or Camp Fire for years. Some parents of my earlier groups did not attend a single ceremonial or potluck dinner or Sunday tea for which the girls had prepared the food. Yet one mother of seven children nearly always managed to attend ceremonies with her daughter. If your time is limited, I would consider the first essential to be attendance at award meetings. A child wants his parents around when he wins recognition or takes part in a program. The teacher or leader would like to meet you and gain a better understanding of your child.

If you can possibly manage it, familiarize yourself with the course of study for your child's Sunday school class. The children whose parents are interested always gain the most from any study.

If you have time for more than attending an occasional meeting and encouraging your child in achievement, there are many small jobs you can do to help the teacher or leader. If you volunteer help instead of waiting to be called, the leader will bless you. Help in transportation enables a group to take many interesting excursions. My husband's Sunday school class was able to visit a Jewish synagogue when the group was studying Old Testament customs and, later in the year, go to Goodwill Industries when the group was learning about

Christian service projects. If he had not had a cooperative group of parents, the children would have missed these excursions.

Perhaps you do not have a car available. Could you help with telephoning if you were given a list? Or could you spend a Sunday morning teaching the group some special craft or skill (related to the lesson) that you have? No leader can be an expert in every field. Frequently the children are called on to help with refreshments at a party or a meeting. Do you see that your child does his share?

Working with children takes time and effort. It is easier to get children to Sunday school than it is to find adequate teachers. Far more children want to join Blue Birds or Scouts than there are leaders available. If your child is lucky enough to have a good Sunday school teacher or belongs to a youth group, see that you do your share. Far more teachers and leaders would volunteer if their jobs were not made difficult by parasite parents.

25

It's Worth the Risk

FAMILY LIFE HAS ITS GREAT MOMENTS and its not-so-great moments. At times when your children are little, life seems an unending procession of diapers, dirty finger marks and spilled milk, but the hard times as well as the good times help cement family loyalties.

Parenthood takes caring and sacrifice; it's more than a birth process. And ironically, joy seems deeper and richer when it is contrasted with some hard times. Our deepest friendships are formed with people who have had similar struggles.

Some people today are afraid to have children. They read all of the statistics about juvenile delinquency or decide that parenthood demands too much of their life. Perhaps they are right for themselves. If you are unwilling to take the time, give the love and discipline and develop the faith to be a parent, perhaps parenthood is not for you. Sometimes people with great career demands or with great causes dominating their lives do not have the time to be parents.

Yet there is risk in everything, and sometimes those who risk the most gain the most. We can read so many statistics about germs or automobile accidents that we can be afraid to breathe or to cross the street.

Over the years the bad moments have become part of the good moments. Now the children delight in recounting the day they and Irving all fell through the ice, but it was terrifying at the time and Kathleen came out sputtering, "I hate Daddy!" They recall the time Irving set the cabin on fire when he tried to change stoves without proper precautions.

Over the years we've made many mistakes, but we've had love, fun, and a common faith in God. There are no people we would rather be with than our children and their mates, and yet we're free to live our lives and they're free to live theirs. We share a common heritage and the deep love of a family that truly enjoys one another.

READING LIST

Books on Philosophy

1. Carrier, Blanche. *Integrity for Tomorrow's Adults.*
   New York: Thomas Y. Crowell, 1959. The emphasis is on responsibility. Character training is
   given more emphasis than individuality.

2. Daily, Starr. *Release.* New York: Harper &
   Bros., 1942. There are days when you will be
   discouraged about your children ever learning
   the difference between right and wrong. Then
   read this story of a hardened criminal who
   turned from crime and hate to God.

3. Edwards, Charlotte. *Heaven in the Home.* New
   York: Hawthorn, 1959. If you have goals outside your family, but your family comes first,
   you'll find this book an inspiration.

4. Frankl, Viktor E. *Man's Search for Meaning.*
   Boston, Mass. : Beacon Press, 1963. Viktor
   Frankl's psychology, hammered out of bitter
   years in a Nazi concentration camp, has far
   more reality for me than Freud's. Frankl in-
   sists that if life has meaning or purpose, we can
   endure difficult situations.

5. Holmes, Marjorie. *I've Got to Talk to Somebody, God.* New York: Doubleday, 1968. Sometimes I feel that no devotional book not written by a mother has relationship to my life. Mrs. Holmes is a good person to read at such a time.

6. Jones, E. Stanley. *Abundant Living.* Nashville: Abingdon-Cokesbury, 1942. I find any of Stanley Jones' books helpful because he emphasizes both the personal and social implications of the Gospel. The organization of daily devotions, bound together by a theme for the year, fits a housewife's busy schedule.

7. Marshall, Catherine. *Beyond Ourselves.* New York: Avon, 1969. Catherine Marshall has a deep, abiding faith, and yet she has had to meet tragedy, disappointment, discouragement, problems of health. Her philosophy has been tested by experience.

8. Miller, Keith. *Habitation of Dragons.* Waco, Tex. : Word, 1970. Miller's honesty about the difficulties of keeping our Christian commitment make his books very practical.

9. Page, Kirby. *Living Joyously.* New York: Rinehart, 1950. I have a strong belief that we can make Christianity attractive to our children if we reflect joy. Kirby Page has emphasis both on helping others and our personal relationship with God.

10. Parker, William R. and St. Johns, Elaine. New York: Prentice-Hall, 1957, *Prayer Can Change Your Life*. At the University of Redlands, Dr. Parker conducted an experiment of using prayer and psychology in meeting problems. The people who used the knowledge of psychology and the power of prayer were most successful.

11. Peale, Norman Vincent. *Enthusiasm Makes the Difference*. New York: Prentice-Hall, 1967. Because mothers frequently have to fight discouragement, Peale's positive approach is very necessary. At times we want to forget the problems of the world and find the answer to our own problems.

12. Schaeffer, Edith. *Hidden Art*. Wheaton, Ill. : Tyndale House, 1971. This book, a Christmas gift from my daughter-in-law, is excellent in showing how the arts and a love of God can be used in transforming even the most mundane task.

Books on Discipline

1. Christenson, Larry. *The Christian Family*. Minneapolis: Bethany Fellowship, 1970. If you believe the father is very definitely the head of the house and there should be very firm discipline, this is the book for you. There are a

number of good ideas here, but for my own philosophy it is too authoritarian.

2. Dobson, James. *Dare to Discipline.* Wheaton, Ill.: Tyndale, 1971. Dr. Dobson's book has a military tinge that occasionally disturbs my pacifist philosophy, but he has some sound suggestions, backed by scientific training. His book would be my first choice for a family that believes in strong parental control.

3. Dodson, Fitzhugh. *How to Father.* Los Angeles: Nash, 1974. This is one of the few books written for the father. Its discipline is basically that of Dr. Gordon, and Dr. Dodson quotes heavily from him. The appendix on crafts, books, etc., is particularly good. Clever illustrations.

4. Gordon, Thomas. *Parent Effectiveness Training.* New York: Peter H. Wyden, 1970 This book promotes neither authoritarianism nor permissiveness, but takes a middle-of-the-road approach. It contains practical information on how to improve communications and how to solve problems when there are conflicts.

Books on Parenting

1. Hoover, Mary B. *The Responsive Parent.* New York: Parents' Magazine Press, 1972. A great deal of common sense is used in writing this

book. Chapters 5 and 6 are good on discipline. There is quite a bit of information on child development.

2. LeShan, Eda J. *How to Survive Parenthood.* New York: Random House, 1965. Although the title is rather negative for the theme of my book, there is a lot of practical advice and good information on the different age groups.

3. Mogal, Doris P. *Character in the Making.* New York: Parents' Magazine Press, 1972. Although the church parent possibly would demand stricter standards in some areas, Doris Mogal has some sound suggestions for developing character. Chapter 5 on responsibility and Chapter 6 on "Everyone Else Does It" are particularly good.

4. Skousen, W. Cleon. *So You Want to Raise a Boy.* Garden City, N.Y. : Doubleday, 1962. This former FBI agent had a large family of both girls and boys. He wrote about boys because more of them tangle with the law. He contrasts two boys who sometimes have similar problems, pointing out which attitudes and reactions could lead to future trouble.